MOVE OUT

MOVE OUT

Michael Duncan

Foreword
by
Stewart Dinnen

STL Books

PO Box 48, Bromley, Kent, England
PO Box 28, Waynesboro, Georgia, USA
PO Box 656, Bombay 1, India

MARC EUROPE

STL Books are published by Send The Light (Operation Mobilisation),
PO Box 48, Bromley, Kent, England.

This is a joint publication with MARC Europe, a ministry of
World Vision of Europe, Cosmos House, 6 Homesdale Road,
Bromley, BR2 9EX, England

ISBN 0 903843 91 9 (STL)
ISBN 0 947697 02 0 (MARC)

Typesetting and page make-up by Mastertype, Bognor Regis, W Sussex.

Cover printed by Penderel Press Ltd., Croydon, Surrey.

Made and printed in Great Britain by Hunt Barnard Printing Ltd.,
Aylesbury, Bucks.

Contents

Foreword

It has been a faith-strengthening experience to watch God's firm hand mould Michael Duncan. I first knew him as a raw, inexperienced convert trying to come to terms with himself and with the new world of Christian values into which he had tumbled.

He could see no other harvest then than the one around him – the needs of other New Zealand young people like himself, just out of the world of drugs and pleasure mania.

It took a year for the vision to widen, but finally a world-awareness burst in upon him. With his sharp intellect and spiritual honesty he was soon motivating others in the same direction.

Even a new phase of pastoral responsibility in a city church did not hinder him from arranging world vision conferences and living a mission-catalyst lifestyle among students and other young people. Incidentally, his church doubled its numbers during that short time.

His book sparkles with spiritual freshness and intellectual vigour. His incisive arguments, backed up by vivid personal experiences, give us chapter after chapter of potent material, capable of prodding the sleepiest, self-centred Christian into wide-awake intensity about God's purpose for strategic living.

He and his wife, Robyn, are currently candidates for cross-cultural ministry overseas. It will be intriguing to see what God does with this young couple.

Stewart Dinnen
WEC International

Acknowledgements

There are many I would like to thank for their support and encouragement. My wife, who has patiently endured many hours of listening to me read page after page to her. Derek and Pam McCormack encouraged me to continue writing, when all I wanted to do was give up. John McNeil edited my final draft; he used his correcting pencil very liberally, but without him and his pen this book would not have been finished. A lot of the typing was done by 'lightning-fingers' Isabel Campbell who over the last three years has done so much to help in the production of this book. My special thanks to Mornington Baptist Church who allowed me to spend some of their precious time on this book. Also, thanks to Hugh Todd for his sketches that so often illustrate what I have been trying to say. My thanks to my publishers who gave me a lot of necessary encouragement from the beginning. Finally, my thanks to men like Murray Robertson, Stewart Dinnen, Evan Davies, Don McKenzie, Alan Shadbolt, Colin Harrington and many others who have ministered to me and helped me grow over the years. To God be all the glory.

All biblical quotations, unless otherwise noted, are taken from the *New International Version*.

Introduction

My wife and I were asked to lead a mission among a group of churches in South West Tasmania, Australia. This involved preaching, speaking at small groups and giving testimonies. We jumped at the opportunity. But what were we to speak about? Having just caught a vision for evangelism we decided to tell these small churches in Tasmania, the smallest state of Australia, that they could have a significant part to play in influencing the world for Christ.

Ants don't move elephants. I was convinced that many of these Tasmanians were going to be sceptical about my message. Surely they would judge me to be a dreamer, a naive, youthful, zealous person who was straight from Bible college. Nevertheless, I did my research and came up with what I thought were pretty good sermons.

Then another problem surfaced. I could exhort them to concentrate on the growth of their church and to evangelise the town, but also to see beyond that to the world and its needs. But after we had left they would probably forget all that had been said. I had to come up with some books that I could leave with them. Books that could explain simply how they could get involved in world evangelism. But despite my searching, I could find none that would inform an individual or church how to take a practical and active part in world evangelism.

So I presented my messages with all the enthusiasm I could muster. There was some good feedback. But then we had to leave and go back to college.

For weeks after this mission I was plagued with one nagging thought. Why was there no book that could explain how normal people like you and me could get involved in reaching the world for Jesus Christ? I took the whole matter to the Lord. After about six months I had the courage and conviction to write such a book.

I was a Christian of only four years. I was in my second year at Bible college and still had so much to learn. Despite these very real limitations I set about doing my research.

It took me three years to write this book. It has been a lot of hard work trying to put my ideas (and those of others) down on paper. But I believe there are some pointers in this book that will help you and your church to get involved in what many believe is God's thrust in the 1980s, world evangelism.

The book is not a theological textbook about why we should get involved in world missions. There are already some very good books on this subject. However, my intention is to give a practical guide on how you or your church can be more effective in world evangelism and discover what God would have you do in world missions today. Since discovering this exciting dimension of the Christian life, the lives of myself, my wife and many others have been changed in so many ways. I want to challenge your thinking and bring about changes in your lifestyle that will serve to extend God's kingdom and glorify him.

Part 1
TAKE YOUR PLACE
IN GOD'S WORLD

1
There Is a Place for You

Home computers, jogging before and after work, drinking wine instead of spirits and reading all the 'get to know yourself' books are some of the new movements our world is telling us to belong to. So what is the new movement of God today? In the 1960s it was the Jesus Movement and community living. Body life and the gifts and person of the Holy Spirit featured in the 1970s. So what is it today in the 1980s? Many believe, as I do, that God's new challenge this decade is to world outreach. Reaching the world for Jesus Christ. Reaching the unreached.

Many are already actively involved in this new thrust in missions. In the United States thousands of young people attend the Urbana student missionary conferences. Just recently a missionary conference was held in Europe and again thousands attended. In my country of New Zealand regional missionary conferences are springing up everywhere. A missionary training college in Australia is having to put people on a two to three year waiting list before they can study there. God is calling to people of all ages and backgrounds to go overseas. Local churches are catching the vision. Giving to missions is on the increase, and all this is just the beginning.

Some may argue that there is no such thing today as a new thrust in missions, and that a missionary emphasis has always been with us and should always be our number one priority. That is true, but just as short hair has been in and out of fashion, so it has been with world outreach. Certainly there have always been pockets of worldwide missionary zeal in all generations since Christ and the first disciples, but church history tells us that certain periods stand out as times in which great advances for the kingdom were made worldwide.

The Early Church (until c.325 AD) crossed many cultural boundaries in its missionary thrust. During the 1500s the Puritans, Anabaptists and the Jesuits among many others travelled far and wide to proclaim the gospel. Many years later, the world witnessed the evangelistic fervour of Count von Zinzendorf and the Moravians. During that same century William Carey came on to the scene. His book *An Enquiry into the Obligations of Christians To Use Means for the Conversion of the Heathen (1792)* did much to promote worldwide missions. During the 1820s and 1830s, interest in overseas missions became a regular feature in church life generally. Missions in the 1980s is again capturing the hearts of young and old alike.

'Michael, what we have got to do today is find out where God is working, grab his "coat-tails" and move with him', said a friend of mine who is soon to go to Manila to work amongst the urban poor. If God is doing a new thing in missions then let's find out what it is and get involved. That is the challenge for Christians and churches in the 1980s.

The challenge

To look at him he was just your average thirty-year-old. His build was not that of Charles Bronson, nor did he come across as the type of person that would win a Superman award. He wasn't pushy, but rather polite and quietly spoken. Yet there was a fire in his bones. These were my first impressions of Viv Grigg. A number of years ago Viv left behind the comforts of New Zealand to go and live among the urban poor in Manila. *The World Christian Encyclopaedia* tells us that the Philippines are 80-90% evangelised[1]. Yet Viv discovered a group of 3,000,000 poor people who were largely being ignored by other Christians. His heart went out to them. He lived among them and witnessed many turning to Christ.

What a challenge — millions of poor people who do not know Christ as their Saviour and Lord. Viv returned to New Zealand to communicate this need to the churches. As a result God has raised up a team of twelve who have committed themselves to live and minister among the poor. Their respective churches have adopted a simpler lifestyle so some of these poor can simply live. Here is a challenge that is beginning to be met.

In eastern Thailand there are 1,500,000 Cambodian-speaking Thai citizens. Only one missionary couple speaks their language and works among them. Here is an urgent need for evangelisation. How many churches, ministers and full-time workers inhabit your area alone? In eastern Thailand there are only two workers among 1,500,000 people.

'New Christians, no teacher'. This was a recent report that came from Guinea Bissau in western Africa. No one could be found to teach and pastor over 300 new Christians[2]. So an urgent plea for a pastor / teacher was sent to the churches and Christians in the West. In some countries there are pastors who teach pastors who teach pastors who finally teach the people! Yet here is a group of people who have no pastor and desperately need one.

Time magazine headlines an article on the world, 'Droughts, Death and Despair'. It goes on to reveal some horrific facts about the plight of the poor in this world. For example, along the 'Street of Sickness' in northern Brazil's sweltering market town of Irauċuba, a family of twelve huddles in a two-room shack, hoping to survive on the £15 a month it receives from the government. Those who take to the road in search of food are no better off. During each of the past four rainless years, as many as 20,000 peasants have abandoned the nine-state north-eastern area of Brazil for crowded urban centres along the coast. There, they are paid 20p an hour and condemned to live in shantytowns[3].

Do we just turn a blind eye to these tragedies? Or do we do as Jesus did? 'For you know the grace of our Lord Jesus Christ, that though he was rich, yet for your sakes he became poor, so that you through his poverty might become rich' (2 Cor. 8: 9). Christ challenges us with his own example, to live more simply so that others may simply live — physically and spiritually. If we accept this challenge our lives will be transformed and we will never regret it.

The challengers

Our world is very much like a lolly scramble. The lollies are the scattered peoples of this world. Just as children rush to get as many lollies as they can, so many groups today are running hard to get as many of the world's different peoples in their grasp. Buddhists, Hindus, Muslims, materialists, atheists, agnostics, Mormons, the Children of God, eastern gurus, drug pushers, hedonists and many others are feverishly trying to convert people to their outlook on life. The world is very much up for grabs.

Communism is leaving its stronghold in Eastern Europe and expanding into Africa, Asia and Central and South America at an alarming rate. An Islamic Missionary Training College in Egypt sends out thousands of firm believers in Mohammed to convert the world. They are very successful. Islam is now the second largest religion in Europe with an estimated 25,000,000 adherents. In Britain alone there are over 300 mosques and 1,000,000 Muslims[4]. Mormonism has of recent years become one of the fastest growing religions.

Election time is always exciting. Some people know who they are going to vote for, but there are thousands of voters who are still making up their minds minutes before closing time. Political commentators on the TV label this group as the 'uncommitted'. Today our world is full of people who do not know whom or what to follow. Between 1976 and 1981 in New Zealand, there was a 66% increase in people who stated they didn't belong to any religion; agnosticism rose by 72% and there was a 174% increase in those who specified no faith at all. It is these uncommitted people who are up for grabs.

This powerful quote in *Time* magazine describes the universal need of this world:

'Before long there will be heard throughout the planet a formidable cry, rising like the howling of innumerable dogs to the stars, asking for someone or something to take command'[5]. (Ortega Y Gasset)

The masses today are like the people Jesus once called 'sheep without a shepherd'. This world is crying out for a leader, and Jesus is alone qualified to fulfil this need. For in Scripture he is described as the King of Kings, the Lord of Lords, the Ruler of all the nations.

Our world needs to hear about the Jesus who came to heal, save and love them. They will only hear if we go and speak to them. Christians are called to be watchmen. The job of a watchman is to warn people of dangers coming their way. The Christian watchman warns of bondage to sin and its subsequent misery. He warns about false religions and points out a way of escape. The watchman has an awesome responsibility. Even though the following passage refers to the watchman of Israel, the principles apply just as much to you and me.

"Son of man I have made you a watchman for the house of Israel; so hear the word I speak and give them warning from me. When I say to a wicked man, 'You will surely die,' and you do not warn him or speak out to dissuade him from his evil ways in order to save his life, that wicked man will die for his sin, and I will hold you accountable for his blood. But if you do warn the wicked man and he does not turn from his wickedness or from his evil ways, he will die for his sin; but you will have saved yourself" (Ezek. 3: 17-19).

A biblical basis for missions

Up to now I have highlighted the need for world evangelism. But it is clear that knowing the need is not enough to motivate Christians to become involved. Many know that thousands are dying each day without Christ but they are doing very little about it. We need to establish the biblical basis for missions in order to understand that along with the need there is also a scriptural mandate for every believer to be involved in missionary outreach. Without a biblical basis it is easy to see involvement in missions as the hobby of a few eccentric enthusiasts.

The biblical basis for missions is rooted in God the Father, God the Son and God the Holy Spirit. The Bible clearly shows that each member of the Trinity has a missionary spirit and purpose.

The living God is a missionary God, who told Abraham that he would bless 'all the families of the earth'. Thus, it is God's intention to bless families in Japan, Indonesia, Italy, Russia, Chile — in the whole world. God promised to bless these families through Abraham's seed (Gen. 12: 3; 22: 18). But who is Abraham's seed? We are, by faith, and the earth's families will be blessed only if we go to them with the gospel. This is God's plain purpose.

The Lord Jesus Christ is a missionary Christ. Jesus is called the light of the world (John 1:9). He came to give himself to the world (John 3:16) in order to be the Saviour of the world (John 4:42). Jesus commands his Church to go into all the world (Matt. 28:19). Jesus came as a missionary sent from God. Now the King of glory sends his Body (believers in Christ) to the uttermost parts of the earth.

The Holy Spirit is a missionary Spirit. The book of Acts has a two-fold emphasis. It is a book about the Holy Spirit, but it is also a book about God's people moving out. There is an inseparable link between the Spirit and outreach. It is the Spirit who convicts the world of guilt in regard to sin, righteousness and judgement (John 16:8). It is the Spirit who empowers believers to be witnesses all over the world (Acts 1:8).

It is the will of each person of the Trinity that the Church not only 'be something' but that the Church also 'do something'. Father, Son and Holy Spirit have created and are building a 'chosen people, a royal priesthood, a holy nation, a people belonging to God'. That is us. But why? 'That you may declare the praises of him who has called you out of darkness into his wonderful light' (1 Pet. 2:9).

How often have you read on dedication, birthday and Christmas cards, 'God be gracious unto you and bless you, and cause his face to shine upon you'? However, this marvellous verse was never intended to be taken in isolation. We must read this verse in context, 'God be gracious to us and bless us and make his face to shine upon us; may your ways be known on earth, your salvation among all nations' (Ps. 67:1,2). God gives to us so that we in turn have something to give to the world. As the song goes, 'Freely, freely we have received; freely, freely give.'

2
Excuses, Excuses

King Saul was an expert at this sort of thing. God commanded him to wipe out the Amalekites, to completely destroy them. He was to spare neither person nor animal. So off he went and defeated the Amalekites. However, he spared the king and some of the best animals. He had disobeyed God's command. Samuel, the prophet, recognised this and rebuked Saul. Saul, however, had his reasons. The best animals were spared so they could be sacrificed to God. He thought he was doing a service to God by not killing everything, as he was commanded to. Now doesn't that sound 'spiritual' of Saul?

Both God and Samuel saw through it. Saul had disobeyed God and it was as simple as that. The real reason why he spared the animals was not because he wanted them as a sacrifice, but because he knew the people wanted them for themselves, and he was too scared to go against their will (1 Samuel 15:24). To get out of his responsibility to keep God's command he thought up an excuse, and clothed it with spiritual jargon, i.e., the need for a sacrifice.

If we want to be free from a certain task or obligation,

then we too will use excuses. I used to be a pastoral worker in a big church with four other pastors, but because I was the junior I was given all the 'dog's-body' tasks — or so I thought. At that time I was not keen on children's work or youth work, but the time came when I had to pull my weight in these areas. Rebellion welled up inside of me. I was sick of doing the jobs I didn't like doing. Self-centredness had become my guide. To get out of the children's and youth work I appealed to all the sound 'spiritual' reasons why I shouldn't be involved. In essence though, they were only excuses.

It may seem strange, but it is usually the things that we try to get out of that end up the most fulfilling things to do. Excuses rob us of so much. Using excuses to get out of world outreach only makes us the losers, for we miss out on much excitement, growth and personal fulfillment. Excuses are robbers and robbers have to be exposed, caught and dealt with. For this reason I have attempted to expose some of the most popular excuses for getting out of world outreach. If some of them sound familiar to you, then deal with them, for in doing so you will gain much.

I am too important

My wife and I moved into a modern, two-storey house ideally situated. We moved our furniture in, and generally tried to make the place comfortable. Slowly but surely the temptation to acquire more than we needed crept into our minds. Thoughts of 'we deserve more' and 'they're *our* lives anyway' predominated. We had begun to think like the world and had ignored the warning in Romans 12: 1,2.

We had begun to think of ourselves. God, however, had a lesson to teach us; that those who seek just for themselves, lose out in the end. The world tells us that if we look after ourselves – Number One! – we will be happy. According to the Lord though, the exact opposite will occur: we will lose much happiness, joy, peace and contentment. God has made us in such a way that true happiness and fulfillment only comes when we look not just to our own interests but also to the interests of others (Phil. 2:4).

The reason that many of us are unhappy, lonely or downright depressed is that we think about nothing but ourselves; *our* wants, *our* hobbies, *our* houses, *our* looks and *our* peace of mind. Even though Christ wants us to extend his kingdom worldwide, it appears that all we want is a marriage partner or a nice home, a good school to send the children to, and more money and time for our pleasures. Many of these things are important, but they're not what life is all about. Being united to Jesus and seeking to further his cause is what it's all about.

Our feelings often tell us to get all wrapped up in our wants, wishes and fancies, but if we let this happen we will surely suffer. Instead, listen to God's word, where he asks us to care about the needy in the whole world. You and I are important, but so are countless others. To Jesus, the starving Ethiopian or the spiritually wayward Hindu are very important — so important that he died for them. We all have a part in reaching these important people and in doing so we will enrich our own lives as well.

All religions lead to the same God

Nick was one of a group of young people who came to our place for coffee and a chat the other night. From the way he was asking questions it was quite evident that he wanted to know what life was all about. His own conviction was that all religions are of equal importance and all lead to the same God. His argument went like this:

'All religions come from the same God and lead to the same God. All the sincere followers in these religions will be accepted by God. Jesus Christ is only one of many. They have Krishna, Buddha, Mohammed; they don't need Jesus. Christians must learn to be accepting and tolerant. It's rude and arrogant to expect that all others must become Christians and believe that Christ is the only way to God'.

This argument seems very plausible. We don't have to be definite about anything. People will like us because we are being tolerant. It all seems like common sense. Why not get everybody's view of God and put them all together to get an overall picture of him? Like pieces in a spiritual jigsaw puzzle it offers world unity and a sense of brotherhood, instead of unnecessary divisions. It also makes world outreach pointless. The idea that all religions lead to the same God is just one big attractive lie.

However, it fails because, firstly, it's illogical. How can all religions lead to the same God when they are all so different? The god of the Hindu is plural and impersonal, the god of Islam is singular and personal. The God of the Bible is the Creator of the world, but the divine in Buddhism is not creative. Salvation for the Buddhist is losing all desire, for the Muslim it is keeping the law, but for the Christian it is knowing Jesus as Saviour and Lord. If all religions come from and lead to the same God then this God must be very confused about himself, the world and man.

Secondly, it's impossible.[1] If it is just up to man to find God then man is doomed to failure. God is too great for finite man to reach. Man cannot reach God through self-effort. In the Bible we see the marvellous picture of God coming down to man in the person of Jesus Christ. If Jesus is equal to Mohammed then, of course, there is no need to convert the Muslim. The Bible makes it quite clear, however, that Jesus is unique, and that he is the only way to the Father (John 14:6). We have got to tell adherents of other religions about him, for their eternal destinies are at stake.

We are all going to heaven in the end anyway
I remember talking to a well educated man in Australia, and he stated quite clearly that he believed all men will be saved. I asked why he believed this. He thought that since God was a God of love he would never condemn people to hell. This implied that everyone is going to be saved in the end therefore why bother to tell people about salvation through Christ?

Some call this line of argument *universalism.* The Bible declares this teaching as wrong. Even though Jesus died for all men, each person can only receive and experience salvation when he accepts Jesus as Saviour and Lord (Eph. 2:8). Hell exists, and those who reject Jesus will go there for eternity (Matt. 7:13; 25:32-46; Rev. 20: 10-15). There is a final judgement. God is going to accept some and reject others (Matt. 25:31,32; 2 Cor. 5:10; Heb. 9:27). God is a God of love. He is also a God of justice (Rom. 2: 5-11), of holiness (1 Pet. 1:16) and of anger (Deut. 13:17). We need to know the God of the Bible and not the god that fits into man-made excuses and schemes.

The day of missions is over
Thousands of Christians are being added to the worldwide Church every single day. Africa and Latin America are forging ahead spiritually. In light of this, is the day of missions over? Is there still a need? Despite the growth in the Third World churches there are still millions who have not heard about Jesus Christ.

Dr. Ralph D. Winter of the United States Center of World Missions, states that to reach the unreached in Africa and Asia alone, we will need one hundred times more missionaries than we are now sending.[2]

Dayton and Wagner, both authorities on mission, have stated that 80% of all unreached peoples will only hear the good news if cross-cultural missionaries are sent to them.[3] Are you still saying there is no need?

It's not my thing
One afternoon I was talking about my convictions on world outreach to a fellow pastor. Early on in the conversation he made his position quite clear. World outreach was simply not his 'thing', but he was pleased that others were involved in it. This attitude is held by many sincere and believing Christians today.

We so often think that world outreach is for the called, the dedicated or the specialist. And, of course, the elderly women! We think that our contribution will make no difference at all. The total cause will hardly suffer because we're not involved. Most of us are leaving world evangelism to the next guy. The end result is that everyone thinks everyone else is doing it and, because of this, hardly anything gets done at all.

World outreach is not an optional extra in God's book – we are all called to be involved in it. Whether we are intelligent or 'dumb', old or young, modern or traditional, rich or poor, God wants us to be involved. The only way missions will become the interest of all people is by missions becoming the interest of believers one by one. So don't wait for others, begin to do your vital bit now.

What about my own 'backyard?'
I will never forget a meeting in which I gave a message on world outreach. Afterwards I made my way to the pew to sit down. Before I got there the minister of the church made an emotional appeal to the members of his church stating that they should care for the needy in their own neighbourhoods before worrying about the rest of the world. He contradicted everything I had said.

It's true, we do need to reach our own neighbours, but let's not stop there. Let's also reach the rest of the world, especially the 3,000,000,000 people who have still not received Jesus Christ. The problem with many of us is that we can't see beyond our own neighbourhood and local church. Jesus wants us to look up (John 4:35) and get involved in other parts of the world (Acts 1:8). A preoccupation with one's own 'backyard' is often just a form of introspection and self-centredness.

Some of the most well known verses in the Bible speak about the world (John 3:16; John 1:29; 2 Cor. 5:19; Matt. 28: 18-20), yet some 90% of all full-time Christian workers are dealing with only 10% of the world's peoples, and only 10% of the workers are working with the remaining 90% of the world's peoples.[5] In the United States – and the figures would proportionally be the same in New Zealand, Australia and Britain – there is one minister to every 400

The Need

CIRCLE ONE: THE WORLD & ITS RELIGIONS

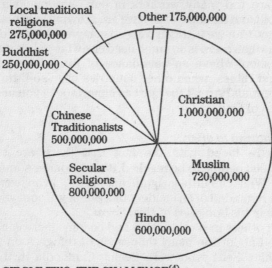

Local traditional religions
275,000,000

Other 175,000,000

Buddhist
250,000,000

Christian
1,000,000,000

Chinese
Traditionalists
500,000,000

Secular
Religions
800,000,000

Muslim
720,000,000

Hindu
600,000,000

CIRCLE TWO: THE CHALLENGE[4]

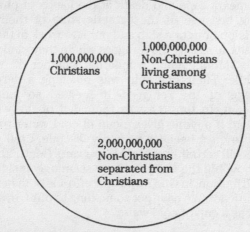

1,000,000,000
Christians

1,000,000,000
Non-Christians
living among
Christians

2,000,000,000
Non-Christians
separated from
Christians

Can we still say there is no need?

people. In many countries, however, pastors are tragically few and far between.

There are too many workers in our own 'backyard'. We're spoilt and because of this we are growing spiritually fat and lazy. Can we justify having so many workers in our countries when there is so much need elsewhere? Is it right that we should have an abundance of food, literature, money and Bibles, when other countries have so little of these essentials? Aren't they just as important as you and I in the eyes of God?

I've got nothing to offer.
When we're faced with the fact that there are still 3,000,000,000 people to be reached, it's no wonder some of us think, 'What can little insignificant me do?' In answer to this, I am reminded of an incident that Stanley Mooneyham describes in his book *Sea of Heartbreak.*

He and others in World Vision had become increasingly concerned about the many thousands of refugees on the South China Seas who were fleeing Cambodia in their makeshift boats in the hope of finding freedom. For many, the trip meant rape and death at the hands of pirates, or drowning because of the pathetic state of their boats. World Vision bought a ship and put it to work in the South China Seas, assisting the refugees where they could.

Stanley Mooneyham wondered whether it was all worthwhile. Their one ship was reaching a very small percentage of the refugees. It seemed so small and insignificant. In time he was reminded of the words of Jesus, 'And if anyone gives a cup of cold water to one of these little ones because he is my disciple, I tell you the truth, he will certainly not lose his reward' (Matt. 10:42). No matter how big the task, and how seemingly insignificant our contribution, in God's eyes our effort is both necessary and significant. We have got something to offer, even if it is as small as a cup of cold water.

The Opportunity

These maps show the worldwide impact that has been made by the preaching of the gospel and, by implication, the areas of challenge where pioneer missionary work is still needed.

MAP ONE: EVANGELICALS WORLDWIDE IN 1780

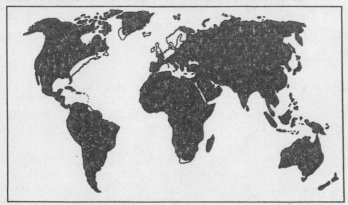

MAP TWO: EVANGELICALS WORLDWIDE IN 1980

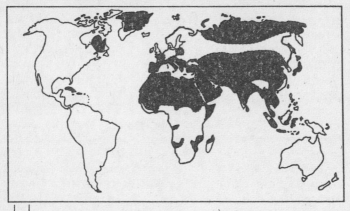

Key

☐ = *geographical spread of evangelical Christians*

Part 2
WHERE IT ALL BEGINS

3
Keeping Jesus First

Cause-centred Christians

Satan will use spiritual causes to keep believers away from Christ. There are Christians who are fired up about apologetics, end-time events, social action, church growth, even missions to the unreached. They are living 'cause-centred' lives. It seems that some Christians will talk about anything but their relationship with the Lord.

Satan is quite happy to divert a Christian's energies into some godly cause. For he knows that the preoccupied Christian who spends little time with his Master will lack the power and life of Christ to be effective in his cause.

'Cause-centred' Christians are breaking the first commandment, 'You shall have no other gods before me' (Deut. 5:7). Gods are not just objects of wood and stone. Money, television, friends, church and causes can so easily become gods. When we live, eat and sleep them, and only give Jesus token recognition, then they are our gods.

Even though I am actively involved in some Christian causes, I know the moment I let them become more important than Christ himself my Christian life will begin to suffer and frustration will take over. We are to be 'Christ-centred' Christians first.

Christ-centred Christians

How do you know whether Christ is first in your life? Ask yourself if you are willing to give up everything else as long as you can keep your faith in Christ? Christ-centred Christians have no problem in affirming with Paul 'I consider everything a loss compared to the surpassing greatness of knowing Christ Jesus my Lord' (Phil. 3:8), and 'For to me, to live is Christ' (Phil. 1:21).

Writing this book became an obsession. I began to think about what I was going to write the moment I woke up, during a shower, over lunch and before I went to sleep. I spent time behind the typewriter when I should have been praying. As a result, I lost some of my zeal and love for Christ. I am now in the process of rectifying this, and I have already begun to see a change in my relationship with Christ.

Why is it so important to be excited about Christ? Apart from the fact that it pleases God, excitement for Jesus is the motivation for missions. When we are excited about Jesus we want to tell others about him. When we lose that excitement our mouths close and our feet come to a standstill. Outreach dies.

I once spent an afternoon building shelves for my office, and I was extremely proud of them. I was so excited — every visitor to our house was immediately informed of every detail of how those shelves were built. It's the same with anything we like. Remember your first bicycle? You couldn't wait to get to school to show it off.

Satan knows that Christians who are not Christ-centred and therefore not excited about Christ will do little or no outreach. He will do anything in his power to bring this about. It is crucial that you keep Jesus Christ as your first love.

Your first love (Rev. 2:5)

The Church at Ephesus had forsaken their first love. God didn't reject them but told them to do three things that would rekindle the love they had lost.

First, they were to 'Remember the height from which they had fallen'. Going back and recalling the good times with Jesus would help them to want those good times again.

Secondly, God asked them to repent; turn away from anything that hindered their relationship with Jesus. It may have been a wrong order of priorities, a failure to forgive self or others, a lack of restitution, living independently of the Holy Spirit, or failure to talk regularly to the Lord.

Finally, they were told 'do the things you did at first'. They remembered the days when they were in love with Jesus. What had they done then to keep their love for him alive? If it were kept alive by prayer, then they had to start praying again. If by obedience, they had to start obeying his commands again, and so on.

I have learnt that when I am finding it difficult to love my wife, waiting to 'feel good' about her doesn't help. It is as I do things for her, like giving her a hug or sitting down for a chat, that my love for her increases. As you *do* what pleases Jesus your love for him will also grow.

God has a place in this world for you, but in the excitement of discovering God's purposes for your life, never forget that his primary purpose for you is to know, to love and to serve Jesus.

4
Becoming a World Christian

A little, run-down house, with cold empty rooms, was the place where I began my spiritual journey. For months I walked in and out of that house agonising over a decision I knew I had to make. Would I allow Jesus Christ to be my Lord? I had just come out of enslavement to drugs, eastern mysticism and the occult. I desperately wanted to change, and Jesus was the key.

On Easter Monday morning 1976 in one of those cold barren rooms, I knelt down and asked Jesus to be my Lord and Saviour. Walking out of that room I knew I was different. Somehow I knew I had begun a new life as a new person. In this book we are also about to embark on a demanding and challenging journey. Up ahead lies the prospect of becoming a world Christian. Those who come along must have as their starting place a relationship with Christ where he is firmly in charge.

Staying in one place can be boring. Some friends of ours have a rule that people who come to stay with them may remain for three days at the most. Beyond that, they have outstayed their welcome. Too many Christians outstay their welcome at the place of conversion. They subsequently never move onto discipleship and new things in God. We have got to come off the commitment mountain and move out onto the plain and make advances for the kingdom. When this happens, we are beginning our journey as world Christians.

Who are world Christians?

Firstly, we can say they're much like anyone else — people who play football, knit cardigans, watch TV, bite finger nails, play darts, ludo, chew gum, struggle to pay the bills and get behind in weeding the garden. World Christians are normal average people.

Secondly, world Christians are not worldly Christians. There is a difference. The former are guided by the will of God, and the latter are dictated to by the things in the world. If you are one, you can't be the other. If you are one, you have no desire to be the other.

I am not suggesting that there are two types of Christians: normal Christians and world Christians. A Christian who sees the world the way God sees it has made a discovery so important that life can never be the same again. Nor is there just one type of world Christian. They come in all shapes and sizes, from many different backgrounds and with a great variety of talents and gifts.

Thirdly, being a world Christian is not a phase. It is a mark of a mature disciple who has caught a vision of the relevance of Christ's death for the whole world.

Being a world Christian can make all the difference

Spiritual growth takes place
Some Christians seem to believe that if they go to meeting after meeting, listen to speaker after speaker and read book after book, they will grow as a Christian. That is only one side of the coin. The other side is equally important, 'Give, and it will be given to you. A good measure, pressed

down, shaken together and running over, will be poured into your lap. For with the measure you use, it will be measured to you' (Luke 6:38). Receiving is not the only way to grow; it is also in giving.

Those who do want to give, often don't know where to give. When we begin to see the world the way God sees it, we begin to notice the poor in Manila, the oppressed in Russia and the suffering in Central America. Suddenly many avenues of exciting giving open up, and as we give sacrificially, God sees to it that we receive what we need to live on and even more to give away.

God becomes a reality

So many Christians complain that God seems far away to them. They rarely see him do anything in their lives. However, as we give to those in need overseas, God will become more real to us. As a young Christian I was told that to see God work I had to be stretched to my limits. I had to put myself in such a position that I was forced to trust God. In my youthful zeal I gave much of my hard earned wages away to missions. It got to a point one week that I had no money to buy a pair of socks. I desperately needed them, so I asked God for a pair of socks. After church the following Sunday, a lady came up to me and handed me a suit. I didn't want a suit, but as I tried it on, I discovered a bulge in one of the pockets — a brand new pair of socks! Whether she had sensed that I needed them because of the smell of the old pair or God had told her, I don't know. But one thing is sure: God became real that day. I had seen him work, and he had answered my prayer. As we help those in need, we are put into situations where we have to trust God or go under. As we see him work, never again can we doubt him.

We have a purpose in life

Psychiatrists tell us that in order to find excitement and fulfillment in life, we need to have a goal, a vision, something to work for and dream about. For the Christian, there can be no greater purpose than the Great Commission of Jesus Christ, to 'go and make disciples of all nations' (Matt. 28:19).

Our priorities become clearer

We all face constant decisions. Should we watch that programme on TV or go to the meeting? Buy a record, or give the money away? Accept the promotion and move, or stay where we are? If our driving ambition in life is to extend God's kingdom worldwide, then such decisions are not difficult. For instance, it will be plain to us that prayer is more beneficial to the kingdom than watching depressing tales on sordid soapies or, if sponsoring a starving child for £7 a month will keep him from dying, then there can surely be no doubt in our minds that this is money well spent as opposed to frittering it away on unnecessary things. To some, this may seem a joyless way to do things, but Jesus said it is more blessed to give than to receive. Even though sacrifices have to be made, we discover an excitement and happiness we haven't experienced before.

We remain steadfast

Peter was unemployed. As I talked to him I was surprised to see how positive and happy he seemed, but as the conversation progressed, I could tell he was bored and tired of just wasting each day. Seeing his depressed state helped me to understand why suicide rates have dramatically increased during the present unemployment crisis.

What about unemployed Christians? The same downward trend occurs. Without a job to do for God, they find Christianity boring. Watching TV and wasting valuable time becomes the norm. They have lost the excitement of being disciples of Jesus, children of the King. Unemployed Christians begin to think they are no good as Christians. Spiritual suicide is the final step — giving up and having nothing more to do with the Christian faith.

That's no exaggeration. Thousands of believers are quite

content to be simply saved. They don't want to serve. They begin to wonder why Christianity doesn't seem to work for them. Finding a job in God's worldwide kingdom, whether it be at home or overseas, is the way to escape this deadly syndrome.

Prayerfully answer the following questions:
1. Is Jesus Christ your Lord, your Boss?
Does he have more say than others, and the final say, when it comes to deciding what to do in your life?
2. Are you bored with being a Christian?
Have you stayed too long on one level, and fallen into a 'spiritual rut'?
Are you willing to be completely open and ask God what is the next step for you? If so, do so.
3. Have you ever thought about the needy in countries other than your own?
Is God speaking to you about exploring this whole dimension of becoming a world Christian?
If so, pray that he will speak to you further as you continue to read this book.

5
Adopting a Simpler Lifestyle

Many sincere and upright believers, when presented with this challenge of world outreach, have chosen to turn their backs on it. Christians have let the world reach them instead of them reaching the world. How has the world reached us? It has done so with its numerous allurements and attractions. A lot of believers have become so caught up with these 'things' that they have no time or energy to take the world for Jesus. They have taken over first place in our lives, so that much of our conversation, time, heart searchings, and arguments are taken up with them. They have become far too important to too many Christians.

What's wrong with having *things?* There is nothing wrong with possessions in themselves, but when we let them consume us, to the neglect of the needy, we place ourselves in dangerous waters. D.L. Moody put it this way, 'The place for the ship is in the sea — but God help the ship if the sea gets into *it*'. Christ commanded us to be in the world but God help us when we let the world get into *us*. The Apostle Paul wisely counsels us, '"Everything is permissible for me" — but not everything is beneficial.

"Everything is permissible for me" — but I will not be mastered by anything' (1 Cor. 6:12).

The *things* must never be allowed to rule our lives. It can be so easy to let the TV programme guide determine our timetable; to see our money vanish on 'hire purchase' payments for things we don't really need and so give nothing to the homeless and starving in the poorer nations; to spend precious hours on a hobby and neglect spending time with the Lord. Contemplate the following narrative, taken from Jamie Buckingham's book *The Last Word*:[1]

'I'm having a hard time enjoying my Filipino houseguest. Already his presence has upset my way of living — a way in which I have grown very comfortable. The alternatives are not pleasant; either get rid of him or change my way of living.

I first met Aley Gonzalez three years before my first visit to the southernmost island of the archipelago: Mindanao. An ex-boxer with more than a hundred professional fights under his bantam-weight belt, this middle-aged, tough-as-coconut-husk, brown-skinned Filipino was preaching like he fought in the ring — both hands jabbing, feet dancing and always boring in for the knockout punch. With the aid of a vintage motorcycle and motorized outrigger canoe, he would go into some of the most inaccessible places in the island chain, starting churches and training pastors.

His average salary was fifty pesos a month (about seven dollars) and his entire wardrobe consisted of three pairs of pants, some shirts, a cheap nylon jacket and a pair of rubber shoes.

Few Americans ever visit his out-of-the-way location in the province of Agusan del Norte. To get there you go seven hundred miles south from Manila, cross two volcanoes, through the straits at Mactan, take a jeep ride through the rain forests to the coastal barrio of Cabadbaran. Those of us who had visited there, however, had encouraged Aley to visit the

States. It would surely broaden his perspective and make him a better preacher. Or, so we thought.

Then Aley arrived at my Florida home. My son Tim had worked that summer and saved money for an expensive new slalom water ski. Knowing how much Aley loved the water (we had spent some happy hours swimming together in the China Sea) I took him with us for a late afternoon ride in our new boat.

On the way to the marina we passed a golf course. "Why do those men hit that little ball with those sticks?" he asked. "Does somebody hire them to do that?"

I started to give him an explanation but realized it sounded foolish, so I stopped. "We have a lot of people in America who do odd things," I mumbled.

Aley nodded. He understood.

"We hear in the Philippines there are many Americans without work. When jobs become more plentiful they will probably stop this foolishness."

I didn't have the heart to tell him that only the rich could afford to be fools.

Aley was impressed with my boat.

"It is very expensive," he said softly, running his hands along the sleek fiberglass deck. "It must have cost twenty thousand pesos. But what do you use it for? Do your sons and daughters fish for a living?"

He could tell I was having trouble with an answer.

"Perhaps you and your wife go up and down the river and preach the gospel to all those out-of-work people swinging their sticks at the balls?" he asked, knowing that somewhere I had hidden a sensible answer.

When I explained we used the boat only to pull water skiers and for some sport fishing, he was startled. I could tell he was thinking of the thirty-two miles he had to paddle his outrigger just to get to the small village of San Jose where he preached the gospel. And here I was with this sleek red-and-white fiberglass beauty. He turned his eyes away and said nothing.

Coming back we stopped at the home of a friend who has three motorcycles in the garage. Aley's eyes danced with excitement, thinking of his battered old Kawasaki.

"These people must go many places helping the poor, feeding the hungry and preaching the gospel," he said approvingly.

When I explained that although these people belonged to the church they weren't active Christians, he was startled. "You have church members who do not preach? How can this be? The Bible says all church members should be preaching the gospel. What then do they use these motorcycles for?"

I explained they were dirt bikes, used only to roar around the woods, going no place. I saw that same pensive look move across his face like clouds over the sun. "There are many things about America which I need to learn," he said, amazed.

I drove home a different way. I didn't want him to see the yachts on the river, the dune buggies in the driveways, or the imposing church buildings which sit idle except for a few feeble groans on Sunday morning. I didn't want to face any more of his questions. It was the same feeling I had many years ago when, as a young idealist, I attended a church service when they dedicated a seventy-five-thousand-dollar stained-glass window — to the glory of God.

But I have mellowed since then. (A state which I imagine Aley would describe as one step removed from going rotten.)

Aley was too kind to say anything to me. But last night I couldn't help but see the expression on his face when he looked in my closet and saw all those shoes.

I haven't been sleeping well recently.'

Many of us could do with such a disturbing house guest. Our lives are cluttered with so many *things* it's no wonder we have no time or energy for world evangelism. There is so much to attend to, investigate, maintain and be involved in that evangelism stays at the bottom of the pile.

We can all remember the depressing times when missionaries have come to our churches and laid the heavy guilt-trip on us! It is as though they have put us in the dock and charged us with such unforgivable sins as hard-heartedness, disobedience and ignorance, for our failure to heed our Lord's command to go into all the world and make disciples. We leave the church feeling condemned and scared of missionaries.

Even though these sincere missionaries have meant well, they have done much to put many off world outreach. Many people are honest when they say they have no time or energy to get involved in world evangelism. They are taken aback when told it's because they are hard-hearted or spiritually immature.

For many of us, it is not spiritual immaturity which prevents us from getting involved in world evangelism. The chief culprit is the cluttered lifestyle we live with its many *things*, demands and pressures: houses, cars, jobs, children, church and finances. They all have to be attended to. There just isn't any time or energy left over for world outreach.

Richard Foster is the author of *Celebration of Discipline* and followed that book with another called *Freedom of Simplicity*. Discipline and simplicity are two necessary ingredients to help us live the lifestyle that makes possible our involvement in world evangelism.

John Wesley was consumed with Jesus Christ. He went out into the fields to preach, and God in his grace brought thousands into the kingdom. In his time he wrote many books and the sales of these earned him hundreds of pounds annually, but he spent only £30 on himself and he gave the rest away. Too often we rush out and buy what we fancy — without consulting our Lord. David Watson had this to say about affluent Christians: 'A very high proportion of Christians in the developed countries are living in comparative gross affluence. We have accepted a lifestyle which is so similar to that of the covetous world around us as to be indistinguishable from it.'[2]

The choice is clear: either we listen to the voice of the advertiser, or we heed the words of Jesus, 'But seek first his kingdom and his righteousness, and all these things will be given to you as well.' The priority is his kingdom not the *things*.

6
Belonging to Others

I had just left behind me the hippie culture with its drugs, eastern religion and long hair. I was sitting by the side of a busy inner-city street watching all the lost and lonely people rush by. I wasn't a Christian but I knew the world was in a mess. The people who passed by had real problems. I didn't know what exactly but I knew they had them.

I was faced with a decision — either run away from the world to live in a rural commune as some of my friends had, or stay and try to help the world I lived in.

The countryside appealed. I could do my own thing and live the kind of life I wanted to live and be who I wanted to be. Staying in the real world to help people was another matter. For one thing, I had nothing to offer. My life wouldn't be my own; it would belong to others. Nevertheless, I chose to stay.

About two years later I became a Christian. The decision I had made previously to give my life to others now became a reality. Jesus Christ as my Lord, claimed my life for his purposes. Christians, as my brothers and sisters, became a very real part of my life. Finally, it was my responsiblity to love and share the Good News with the lost. My life now belonged to the Lord, to Christians and to the unbelieving world. This kind of lifestyle has not been easy at times, but I have never regretted it.

Belonging to the Lord

According to the South American pastor Juan Carlos Ortiz, a disciple is 'Someone who follows Christ. . . . And following Christ means acknowledging Him as Lord. It means serving Him as a slave. It means change, to grow and move from the baby days which many have prolonged.'[1]

Many accept Jesus as their Saviour, the one who can forgive, heal and transform them, but few actually experience his saving grace in their lives. Jesus Christ will never become our day-to-day Saviour unless we make him our Lord first of all.

For example, Christ the Lord may see that our thought-life needs to be dealt with. He tells us so. If he is our Lord, then in obedience we will allow him entry into this area to do what he thinks best. If he is not our Lord, we may choose to ignore his voice and let our mental habits remain as they are. Therefore we do not experience his saving grace. If he is not our Lord we will usually end up refusing him entry into our lives as Saviour. As a result we will be denied so much blessing.

Pastors and evangelists often invite people to allow Christ to be their Lord. Scripture also makes it plain that people are not only invited, but commanded, to make Christ their Lord. His lordship is not optional — it is a command. Both unbelievers and believers have an obligation to make Christ Lord for the following two reasons:

Firstly, he is the Creator (Gen. 1; John 1: 1-10). If I make a table then that table belongs to me. The created object belongs to the Creator. So it is with Christ. He created mankind and therefore we, as his creation, rightfully belong to him. He is the rightful owner and he has the right to do what he pleases with us. He is the Lord.

Secondly, he is our Redeemer: 'You are not your own; you were bought at a price. Therefore honour God with your body' (1 Cor. 6: 19,20). He purchased us with his blood. When I go into town and buy a record, then that record belongs to me. I can do what I like with it: play it softly or loudly; play it weekly or just twice a year; keep it or smash it. When our eyes were opened to the fact that Christ purchased us with his blood and we accepted that, then as the purchaser he also became our owner. He can do whatever he likes with us. 'And he died for all, that those who live should no longer live for themselves but for him who died for them and was raised again' (2 Cor. 5:15).

Let us not just be content with being church members, pew-fillers, hymn singers, sermon tasters, Bible readers, born-again believers – or even Spirit-filled charismatics! Let us rather become true disciples – with Jesus as Lord, and with hearts willing to learn and obey.

Belonging to other believers

A young man left his home country of Germany and went to Indonesia as a missionary. At the outset he was put in the care of an older missionary. Everything that the older missionary did — he had to do. Everywhere the older missionary went — he had to go. His job was to do what he was told, without question. For a number of years his life was totally involved in that of the older man. He had no opportunity to act independently.

Ask a Christian today to be interfered with like that and he will refuse. 'How dare someone interfere with me like that. What right has anyone to dictate to me what I should and shouldn't do!!' You see, the young man had discovered a secret that was to change his life. By allowing the older man to interfere, he learnt so much. His character changed. He became less and less self-orientated, and as a result God could use him.

In the New Testament the word *disciple* means, to be a learner. A learner must be open to truth. Truth about himself, his weaknesses, ministry and lifestyle. A disciple is prepared to be interfered with — to learn from others and the Lord Jesus.

If we are not prepared to be told what to do, then God will not use us in his world. If we want a ministry of warning non-Christians about their spiritual state, then first of all we have got to be open to Christians warning us about the way we are living. If we want to be straight and honest with others, then we've got to let others be straight and honest with us.

I only have the ministry I now have because others had the courage to interfere in my life – and I let them. It wasn't easy at times. There were many misunderstandings and heartaches. Heated arguments and raised voices also featured. On most occasions I found it humbling and even humiliating, but 'Those who sow in tears will reap with songs of joy' (Ps. 126:5). I am so glad now that I went through those times, for personal growth has resulted. Now this is a clear biblical principle, 'Instead, speaking the truth in love, we will in all things grow up into him who is the Head, that is, Christ' (Eph. 4:15).

As others speak the truth (about me) to me, I will grow up and become more Christlike. Again, in the Old Testament, 'As iron sharpens iron, so one man sharpens another' (Prov. 27:17). If we are willing to learn from others and be interfered with, then the rough edges of the 'old man' will be knocked off, and in their place the fruit of the Spirit will emerge.

To see this happen I suggest you spend more time with the 'difficult' people in your life. Instead of running away from people you can't stand, befriend them and if you can, invite them home for a meal. Let them become a part of your life. Secondly, if you have a tendency to be a lone ranger in your decision-making, begin asking people for their advice and opinions. Finally, when you are asked to do something you don't feel like doing — do it. It will be difficult putting into practise these suggestions. They do go against the grain. You will need the Holy Spirit and as you depend upon him he will change you.

Belonging to the lost

God's smuggler, Brother Andrew, was watching a television film in England about the 'Great Leap Forward' in China. It showed the Chinese working like slaves in order to overtake Britain as an industrial nation. As Brother Andrew watched he was so taken with the fact that millions of Chinese were ignorant of Christ that he began to weep uncontrollably.

Tears are not fashionable today. They are something to be ashamed of. A man who cries is weak-kneed and feminine. Or so our world tells us. But in the Bible tears are a sign of strength and maturity. David, the Psalmist, (and a man's man at that), tells us that tears can be the beginning of something great: 'Those who sow in tears will reap with songs of joy. He who goes out weeping, carrying seed to sow, will return with songs of joy, carrying sheaves with him' (Ps. 126: 5,6).

Brother Andrew sowed tears the night he watched that programme. Today he is reaping joy. Through his ministry of Open Doors, thousands of Chinese are being reached for Christ. Thousands are receiving a Bible for the first time. Never be ashamed of tears. Never run away from them. For they may, as in Brother Andrew's case, lead to something great.

Tears reveal a compassionate person, but tears alone will accomplish little. They are only the beginning. Jesus was a compassionate person. In fact, the supreme motive behind Jesus' service was compassion. With his eyes he saw the needs of others. His heart ached for them. So with his life he served them. His compassion led him to go to the needy, to heal, teach, feed and transform them. His compassion was genuine and not superficial. His compassion compelled him to action. There is no compassion where there is no action. The two always go together. It has to be the same with us. Feelings of compassion aren't enough. The thousands who are dying right now without Christ are not interested in our feelings, only in our actions. Only by our actions will we reach, feed, heal and speak the Good News to them.

So, how does one become a compassionate person?

Know God's heart

The more time I spend with my wife, the more sensitive I become to her feelings. Discovering how another person really feels, reacts and thinks, takes many intimate hours. So it is with our heavenly Father. Prayer and Bible study reveal the heart of God to us. Through spending time with him, we begin to sense how he is feeling and grieving over the lost and needy in this world. In time, his heart becomes our heart.

Know who and where the needy are

Three out of four people on this earth still don't know Christ. About 80% of them will only be reached by cross-cultural missionaries. Will they have that opportunity to listen? In Ethiopia, in 1973, over 200,000 people died in a drought. Did they die knowing Christ? Half the world's population — 2,000,000,000 — are under-nourished. In Latin America 50-75% of the deaths of children under the age of five are due to malnutrition.[2] Surely, these children are too young to die?

Not long ago I read these facts about real people and I began to cry. Some days later I made a decision to do what I could to help the suffering overseas. My wife and I adopted a simpler lifestyle so we could give more. We started to pray more for other countries. We told others about the plight some foreign peoples are in today. Many Christians in the West, quite understandably, never see or come into contact with serious human suffering. Because of this the 'out of sight – out of mind' attitude prevails. Or it could be that we see so much suffering on television or in the newspapers that our senses are dulled by it.

For this reason, as we research our world and keep in contact with it, we need to pray that God will speak to us through the suffering we see. Our televisions and radios vividly portray the lifestyles some people are forced to endure in this world. We can either put up our defences and become indifferent to what we see and hear, or we can try to discover what God wants us to do to rectify what we see and hear.

Know what it means to suffer

I am not suggesting that we all inflict pain on ourselves. Nor am I asking us to live the rest of our days like hermits. Rather, try living on rice for a day or two and begin to experience what hunger is like. For one week say 'no' to everything you want to buy. Begin to know what it feels like to be deprived of things. Sleep on the floor one night instead of diving into bed. These suggestions are short-term experiments. For a brief period we can attempt to put ourselves in the shoes of the deprived overseas.

'This is how we know what love is: Jesus Christ laid down his life for us. And we ought to lay down our lives for our brothers. If anyone has material possessions and sees his brother in need but has no pity on him, how can the love of God be in him? Dear children, let us not love with words or tongue but with actions and in truth' (1 John 3: 16-18).

7
Being Spirit-Filled

My reason for taking drugs was to get some answers to my questions. Instead of answers — confusion and further doubt filled my mind. So I turned to eastern mysticism, yoga and meditation. I thought these would change me as a person. They did, but it was a change for the worse. They destroyed my personality. Not finding the answers I wanted, I again became extremely frustrated with life.

> Frustration is to be a lion,
> Starved and captive. Then
> the trap door opens, and
> there's a Daniel in your den.[1]

Christians do not escape from frustration. Many of us are like the lion. We want something, indeed need something, but somehow we don't get it. We yearn to hear God's voice. We want to give away our faith to unbelievers. We wish we could only stop doing those things that hinder our relationship with God. We know we ought to be world Christians but we just can't be bothered. There is much we want to attain, but all we seem to do is miss the mark. Frustration roars within.

The Apostle Paul describes his own sense of frustration:
'I do not understand what I do. For what I want to do I do
not do, but what I hate I do . . . For I have the desire to do
what is good, but I cannot carry it out. For what I do is not
the good I want to do; no, the evil I do not want to do — this
I keep on doing . . . What a wretched man I am! Who will
rescue me . . . ?' (Rom. 7:15-25).

The Holy Spirit is the answer. Romans 7 speaks about
frustration, and in the following chapter Paul talks of the
Holy Spirit. It is he who can transform frustration into
fulfillment. The Bible makes it quite clear that all self effort
is doomed to failure. The moment we try to attain all that
God has for us – by ourselves – we put ourselves on the
road to failure and frustration. We can only do God's work
with God's power. It is impossible to be a Christian without
relying upon the Spirit of God.

Many know that God's Spirit is needed and dwells within
them. Yet, they say, he seems to be making no difference at
all. He is only a 'sleeping partner'. Here are three
suggestions to rectify this situation:

Firstly, see yourself as spiritually poor. We are often
tempted to think that we are okay, and that we have got
what it takes to be a Christian and make things happen. In
this condition we resemble a glass full of rubble instead of
water. Water cannot be poured into a glass filled with
something else and God cannot pour his Spirit into us when
attitudes of complacency and self-satisfaction prevail. God
wants us to be spiritually poor – to know our emptiness.
(Matt. 5:3; Ps. 86:1; Heb. 4:16).

Likewise, our missionary programmes can be chosen,
directed and terminated by ourselves. For this reason it is
no wonder that many such programmes in our churches
are in pieces — resembling rubble. We need to be positively
dissatisfied with where we are in relation to the missionary
front. In our dissatisfaction we must turn to God's Spirit to
guide us in his (not our) mission.

Secondly, see yourself as utterly dependent upon him.

Have you ever watched a doubles tennis match, where one of the partners darts all over the court chasing each ball. In doing so, he renders his partner redundant. We can be like that with the Holy Spirit. Whenever a problem comes our way we dart in and try to sort it out. The Holy Spirit is treated as a by-stander. So it is no wonder we never see him at work in our lives. Instead, we need to give him room to act, by waiting patiently and letting him make the first move.

In this day of umpteen dozen missionary organisations, Christians and churches alike face a confusing task deciding which missionary or mission to support. We need to be discerning, rather than rushing in and supporting what seems right, when in the sight of God it is not (see John 15:5; Gal. 3:3).

Thirdly, see yourself under the lordship of Christ. Disobedience puts a barrier between us and the Holy Spirit when we neglect, disregard or despise what he asks. Scripture tells us we can 'put out the Spirit's fire' (1 Thess. 5:19), i.e. hinder and thwart what he is trying to do in our lives.

In Ephesians we are told that we can so easily grieve the Spirit. The word *grieve* means to be vexed, or to be at cross-purposes with the Spirit. He wants to go one way and we want to go the other way. When three or four young people live in a flat together, they are usually in for the surprise of their lives. Initially the prospect of living together in the same house seems exciting, but in time they discover how difficult it is. So it is with us and the Holy Spirit. He is a real person. He has come to live in our house (our lives). We now have to learn to live with another in us, and obedience to this divine inhabiter is the only way to successfully accomplish this. The more we agree with him the closer we will get to him.

We have established that the Holy Spirit is given to us so we can live the kind of lives God wants us to live, but is he given so that only you and I might benefit from his power? Definitely not!

Buying books is a real weakness of mine. I try to read at least one a week. A while ago I went into a bookstore that is known for its emphasis on the Holy Spirit. From the moment I stepped in all I could see were books about *my* peace, *my* joy, *my* growth, *my my my* ad infinitum. The store was full of *me* books and communicated *me* worship. I had to go to a hidden corner in the back of the store to find some books on outreach! We have forgotten who the Holy Spirit is and why he has come.

Most will recognise that there has been a move of God's Spirit worldwide in the last twenty years or so. Much good has come out of this new move of the Spirit, but sadly this movement has let a dangerous emphasis of self-worship become a dominant feature. Many are preoccupied with their own froth and bubble experiences. 'Me'-thinking Christians and self-centred churches are a by-product of this. To overcome some of these exaggerated emphases we need to look afresh at who the Holy Spirit is.

The Holy Spirit is a Spirit of *servanthood.* A lot of pastors and authors today present the Spirit as the pathway to power in one's life, to success and ecstatic experiences. They are right, but they have stopped there, limiting the Holy Spirit. He also indwells us so that we might be effective servants to Jesus and to others. Being a servant is a humbling and difficult task. So it is in this area especially that we need the aid of the Spirit.

Paul was a Spirit-filled man and described himself as one who was: condemned to death, a fool, weak, without honour, hungry and thirsty, roughly treated, homeless, slandered, persecuted and the scum of the world (1 Cor. 4: 8-13). I am not suggesting that all of us will be called to live like that, – just because he was filled with the Spirit didn't guarantee that everything in his life would be rosy. For him, being Spirit-filled meant being a servant, and a suffering one at that. We too, are indwelt by the Spirit, so that we might serve the needy, whether they be our neighbours or persons overseas.

The Holy Spirit is a Spirit of *mission.* He has come to

equip us for outreach. I agree with the words of David Watson, 'Any claimed experience of the Spirit which does not enrich the missionary and evangelistic work of the church is suspect.'[2] Acts is a book about the Holy Spirit. It is also a book about God's people moving out. We cannot separate the Spirit from outreach. So often we grieve the Spirit beccause we ignore or even disapprove of the missionary zeal that some are trying to establish in our churches or groups. Michael Green, when talking about the Spirit, states that the Comforter comes not in order to make us comfortable, but to make us missionaries.[3]

The key marks of a Spirit-filled man are not that he speaks in tongues or has a word for someone. These are valid and helpful gifts, but a Spirit-filled man or woman is one who stoops to serve, and has a passion to see unbelievers come out of the kingdom of darkness into the glorious kingdom of God.

Whenever there has been a genuine move of God's Spirit in church history, serving agencies and missionary organisations have emerged from it. God's Spirit moved powerfully through the ministries of Charles G. Finney and Dwight L. Moody. Out of these or similar revivals sprang the World's Student Christian Federation, the Salvation Army, the Young Men's Christian Association, Christian Endeavour, the Sunday School, the Church Missionary Society, and the Free Church of Scotland with its strong foreign missions emphasis. When the Spirit moves he produces servants and missionaries.

God has been graciously pouring out his Spirit on many countries around the world. People and churches are being renewed in the power of the Spirit and because of this we are seeing a renewed interest in missions. Young people from all over are attending mission camps and conferences. For example, many of the charismatic churches in New Zealand are being burdened by the plight of the poor in South East Asia. Teams are being sent out to live amongst the poor in Manila and other slum areas. Spirit-filled Christians are willing to be servants to the poor so that some may turn to Christ.

'The Spirit of Christ is the spirit of missions, and the nearer we get to him the more intensely missionary we must become'.[4]

8
The Enemy Is Near

Nothing good comes without a fight. My wife and I have been married now for about three years. It is very hard to find the words that can adequately describe the goodness there is in marriage. Contentment, pleasure and fun would be some of them, but these benefits didn't just come with a flick of the fingers, we had to work for them. In our first year of marriage we encountered enemies like pride, selfishness and anger that sought to destroy our developing marriage. Something that is good never comes cheaply or easily.

It's the same with world outreach. God is pleased with it, people are helped and we ourselves are fulfilled in it. Endeavouring to be a world Christian or to set up a world outreach operation in your church will not be easy. There is an enemy who will do everything possible to discourage us, and to destroy all that we do. Satan is not bothered about comfortable Christians who keep their faith to themselves, but he gets incredibly angry with those who seek to proclaim their faith to the uttermost parts of the earth. He is their enemy.

Last night I was watching a film on the life of Ike Eisenhower, the Allied Commander in charge of ridding the Middle East of Rommel and his German forces, during the Second World War. By way of preparation, he obtained an autobiographical account by Rommel, and read it from cover to cover. He wanted to know how the man ticked, so he could attempt to predict his movements. This preparation paid off because the allies under Ike defeated their enemy. As we endeavour to be a world Christian involved in world outreach, we will be attacked by Satan. To defeat him we need to know how he operates. The best way to do this is to discover what Scripture has to say about his character. Firstly, Satan is described as a *tempter.* His plan is to persuade us to take an alternative course to God's way (Luke 4: 1-13; 1 Thess. 3:5). While God is telling us to get involved in world outreach, Satan may subtly persuade us to channel all our energies into a new building programme.

He is also a *liar* (John 8:44, Acts 5:3). He may instill in our minds one or all of the excuses described in chapter 2, so that we become genuinely convinced that world outreach is no longer needed or possible.

Then Satan is described as an *ensnarer* (1 Tim. 3:7) and *accuser* (Rev. 12:10). He is out to trap the Christian to sin, so that his testimony is spoiled. Satan knows that a disobedient believer is not an effective worker for God. Not only this, but as the devil, he loves to throw people's misdeeds back at them. Even though we may have been forgiven for something that we committed in the past, he will bring it up again, in order to condemn or discourage us.

As the *hinderer* he seeks to put things in the way of the Christian who is seeking to do God's will (1 Thess. 2:18). How many times have you heard about a promising candidate for some ministry who suddenly gets entangled in a business venture, or with a girl, and soon finds himself unwilling or incapable of doing God's will?

Then, as the *oppressor* he uses depression and discouragement as weapons to undermine the Christian's sense of purpose (1 Kings 19).

As the *troubler* Satan seeks to invade the physical realm and to limit the effectiveness of God's children (2 Cor. 12:7). If he can't trap you in sin or bind you mentally, then the body is his next obvious target.

Finally, Satan is the *creator of division.* The blessing of God will not be found where there is dissension. God's work is so often hindered because we fail to agree on a course of action. Behind this apparent human situation is Satan (2 Cor. 2: 10,11).

How do we fight such a menace? There have been countless times in history, when leaders have ordered their men armed with only spears and swords to attack their enemies armed with guns. The sword carriers didn't have a chance and they might just as well have committed suicide. Our God is not like those leaders: he doesn't command us to fight an enemy certain to defeat us. From his word comes the command to fight Satan, but from that same word, he also tells us how to defeat Satan.

From a pamphlet entitled *31 Tips on how to Recognise and Resist Satan,* written by Stewart Dinnen, comes the following scriptural basis for overcoming Satan.

Scriptural basis

1. If you are a new creature in Christ you have been brought out of Satan's dominion (Rom. 6: 1-14; Eph. 2: 1-10; Col. 1: 13,14; 3: 1-3).

2. Satan's power in human life was broken at the cross and in the Resurrection (Rev. 12: 10,11; 1 John 3:8b; Heb. 2: 14,15).

3. Your position is described in Romans 8:37 as a super conqueror and in Revelation 1: 5,6 as a king-priest, sharing Christ's authority and standing.

4. Stand in total faith on the finished work of Christ (1 John 3:8b) and the power of your new relationship in him (2 Cor. 5:17).

5. Christ taught the possibility and necessity of 'binding

the strong man' (Mark 3:27), i.e. asserting our authority over him in Christ and denying him freedom of action in a given situation.

How can I overcome him?

1. Submit yourself unreservedly to God's will, and that means in everything (James 4: 6,7).

2. Wear the full armour (Eph. 6: 11-17). If you don't understand what the armour is, then obtain a good book on spiritual warfare that will shed some light on the subject.

3. Maintain a vital walk with God through the weapon of constant prayer (Eph. 6:18; 1 Thess. 5:17).

4. Resist Satan and he will flee from you as directed in James 4: 6,7; 1 Pet. 5: 8,9; Eph. 4:27.

5. Rely on the cross-work of Christ. Jesus overcame Satan and rose in victory (Col. 2:15).

'They overcame him by the blood of the Lamb and by the word of their testimony' (Rev. 12:11).

9
Guidance

A question

Guidance starts when we begin to ask questions. God's answers will come if we want to know them. Brother Andrew states that the secret to success lies in the ability to ask questions. He says the courage to ask questions will change your life.[1]

Why is there so much suffering in this world? What is God doing about it? What does God want me to do? Where does he want me to go? These are questions we must ask. The answers will only come when we mean business with God, when we genuinely want to discover his will.

Brother Andrew was a student at the College of the Worldwide Evangelisation Crusade in Glasgow, Scotland. Visiting missionaries from all over the world would come and lecture about their fields. Eventually Brother Andrew asked a question that was to change his life: 'Have any missionaries come from the communist countries?' The answer was 'No'. It began to dawn on him that millions of people in communist lands were living and dying without ever having heard the good news about Jesus Christ. Something had to be done. Since then God has done great things through this man and others of the Open Doors team to reach thousands for Christ. And it all began with a question.

A survey was taken in Australia among Christian students to discover why so few were entering mission-orientated work. For a lot of the students, consulting God about their future was just a waste of time. Instead, they consulted the world. The world told them 'do your own thing', and 'if it feels good — do it'.

A lot of us are not consulting God about our future because we are not too sure whether we can trust him. Will he really guide me? Does he know what's right for me? The confidence to trust God will only come as we get to know him more personally. It's the same with any relationship, the more you know a person, the easier it is to trust him.

I would hardly entrust £1000 to someone I did not know, but I would give it to my best friend. I know I can trust him because I have spent time with him. It is the same with God. The more we spend time with him in prayer and Bible study, the more we will get to know him as trustworthy. But even when I have learnt this how do I get my guidance?

While I was a pastoral worker in a big church I found it extremely difficult to get close to people, or to let them get close to me. The problem was undercutting my ministry. So I was forced to ask, 'What is to be done about it?' The answer changed my life: 'Go to the WEC International Bible College in Tasmania, Australia'. My two years there not only changed me as a person, but also gave me a whole new dimension on the world. It all started with a question.

The saga of guidance

If you find guidance a struggle, be encouraged, so do I. I have no secret formula to pass on to you. I don't believe there is one. The lessons on guidance I have learnt have come through the hard school of experience.

I will start with my marriage. Eight years ago Robyn

walked into my life at a home group meeting. From that moment on I couldn't get her out of my mind. God, is this the girl for me?

Robyn – wanting some guidance on our relationship – went to stay with a friend in the country. While there she believes God gave her a dream, in which we were serving the Lord together. But it was two years after the dream that we were finally married. When God says he wants us to do something, he doesn't necessarily mean straight away. It is one thing to know what God wants us to do, it is quite another to know when.

At the time I met Robyn I was working in a paper bag factory. After two years there I was asked by my church to become one of their pastoral workers. Six months into the job everything fell apart: Robyn and I broke up; I had to vacate my flat; my part-time gardening job came to an end; and I was having a few personal problems with the church leaders (all my fault!).

'Have you considered going to a Bible college?' a friend asked.

'No. And I don't want to!' I barked back. She persevered and told me that the Missionary Training College in Australia would be ideal for me. She herself had been there.

Eventually, walking to church one day I asked the Lord whether he wanted me to go. Right then and there I believe he spoke to me. His voice wasn't 'spooky', harsh or strange. It was a perfect blend of love and authority. It came from within my spirit. It wasn't an impatient or demanding voice. I was spiritually uplifted after hearing it. Most important was the clear and specific direction, 'Go to college now'.

That was in May. I rang up Stewart Dinnen, the Principal of the college. 'Come now,' he said, 'we have a new intake in three weeks' time.' That same day my pastor got back to me and told me the elders were all in favour. Three weeks later I was sitting in a lecture room.

Circumstances, friends, God's direct voice and elders were all used to guide me to college. God is a God of variety. There are many ways in which he can speak:

dreams, visions, prophecies, Scripture, signs, elders, pastors, preachers, circumstances and even common sense can be used by God to speak to you. Don't lock God into one way of speaking. Be open to any way(s) he chooses to use.

Although guidance to go to college was clear, what to do after graduation was another matter. We could either stay at college another year so Robyn could complete her course (she had joined me at the end of my first year) and then go overseas. Or we could go back to New Zealand to pastor a church. Despite much praying, fasting and debating, no guidance came. On the last day of college the heavens were still silent. We decided to come back to New Zealand because it appeared the choice was ours.

I do not believe there is only one right way. God is a big God. If we sincerely want to follow his will, I don't believe he will let us make an irreparable mistake. He loves us too much for that.

After we had spent three years of ministry back in New Zealand, God quite clearly told us that we were to start heading overseas . . . but where did he want us to go?

After consulting a mission leader, three options were suggested. The first was a two-year commitment as a travelling evangelist, pastor and teacher with groups of young people throughout the Mediterranean. This appealed, we applied and were accepted. However, after all this had been finalised, I became uneasy about it. I sensed it wasn't the right mission or ministry for us. I wrote and apologised and asked them to withdraw my application.

The second option involved going to the Gambia in West Africa. Believing this would give us real grassroots missionary experience, we applied to join WEC International. And then it happened again — we met a missionary friend who had just returned from the Gambia, and after talking to him it became clear that this wasn't the right place either.

By this time we were getting confused and frustrated. Some of our friends were giving us the 'raised eyebrows'.

Did we know what we were doing? Why were the Duncans changing their minds so much? Have they done the right thing in deciding to leave the ministry in New Zealand?

Then the totally unexpected occurred. The Principal of the Missionary Training College in Australia asked me to consider joining the staff as a lecturer. This appealed to us as we yearned to see young people go overseas. I informed the Principal that we were working on coming. We were relieved to know what we were finally going to do.

There was one problem though. How could we teach and train prospective missionaries when we had no cross-cultural experience ourselves? It niggled us so much that we realised it was another caution. By this time I had become an expert at writing 'humble-pie' letters. The Principal was sent one, telling him that I was not coming.

None of the options worked out. God used an uneasy feeling, the counsel of a friend and a good question to stop us in our tracks, but why didn't God come straight out and show us where he wanted us to go? We could have been spared a lot of mistakes and heartache.

One step did become clear. We were to join WEC International. Three months later we were doing their orientation course.

Investigating those three options had taken one year. It wasn't wasted time. God is never in a hurry. His way is step by step. Before he was going to reveal the 'where' he wanted to clarify the 'why' and the 'what'. Why did I want to be a missionary? It was a time to be honest. I wanted to have the right ministry overseas only so I could be self-fulfilled. I was looking out for my interests, not the interests of those to whom I was going. My 'why' had to change.

What was to be my ministry overseas? I wanted to be the popular 'platform speaker'. Speak in churches, at student camps and conventions, etc. God didn't agree. He asked me to give up all my ambitions and dreams. As a very ambitious person I found this extremely difficult, but with tears I did.

With an empty heart God now had room to deposit his

own desires and plans. Very slowly a vision for evangelism, church planting and church growth in the big cities of Asia began to emerge.

God is not ruled by our guidance formulas. We cannot press a button to get the right answer. We are to put our faith in God, not guidance. We are to seek God, not guidance. Guidance is a relationship with God, not a set of equations.

In our seeking, we must not be rude to God. For many months I arrogantly came to God and demanded that he reveal to me his will. One day I got the distinct impression he was asking me to be quiet. To stop rambling on about guidance. As I knelt it suddenly dawned on me that I didn't deserve a thing from him. Guidance wasn't mine to demand, but it was his to graciously give.

He has indeed been gracious, as he has guided us through a number of issues. We have been overwhelmed at his goodness and his love. God knows our future and that's all we need to know.

If we are seeking to become involved in some ministry, God may give guidance in a variety of ways; perhaps through reading the Bible, seeing the needs of the world, hearing mission reports or going through a crisis experience. Let us not forget though an important biblical principle: the role that others around us play. Your call is not simply a matter between you and God. Michael Griffiths has this to say:

'Not one of the New Testament missionaries whose call the Holy Spirit has recorded in the Acts of the Apostles went out on his own initiative or in response to his own subjective sense of calling alone. In most cases, the subjective sense of call, though it may have been present, is not mentioned and is not the aspect of the call to which the Holy Spirit chose to draw our attention. In every case either the church with which they were associated or a missionary familiar with the work had a considerable part to play. In other words, the objective call is stressed more than the subjective sense of calling' (Acts 11:22,25; 13:2; 15:40; 16:3)[2].

Today many are rushing around seeking God's call for their lives and seem to be getting nowhere. Maybe, if they spent more time listening to their pastors, elders, parents and other Christian leaders, their seeking would prove more profitable.

Even though the recommendations of others have not always proved right for us, we still value highly the counsel and input from respected friends and leaders. We will always seek their opinions. There is safety in a multitude of counselors. Any Christian going it alone is taking an enormous risk.

If you feel you have had an answer from God, I encourage you to consider the following questions:

1. Does it agree with God's general plan as set forth in his Word?
2. Do your circumstances agree with what seems to be his leading?
3. Does the Holy Spirit bear continual witness that this is the will of God?
4. Are you still called when there is no challenge of adventure and no glamour of heroism?
5. Are you willing to pay any price?
6. Is it a mere impression, or a deep conviction?[3]

Suppose we believe we have the call of God, apply for the position – or make appropriate steps in the right direction – and then either get turned down or things don't turn out? Don't automatically slip into the valley of despair. God's ways of getting us somewhere are not always our ways. Remember, one closed door may lead to an open door later on. God has his own timing and sequence; our job is to trust him.

Home or overseas?

Elizabeth Elliot knew that Jim, her husband, would be leaving without her on his missionary trip to South America, and so she began to discuss with him the possibility that he would not return.

'If God wants it that way, darling', he said, 'I am ready to die for the salvation of the Aucas.'

He and four other men sat together on a strip of white sand on the Curaray River, deep in Ecuador's rain forest, waiting for the arrival of a group of men whom they loved, but had never met — savage stone-age killers. On 8th January 1956, the men for whom Jim Elliot had prayed for six years killed him and his four companions.

In her book *Shadow of the Almighty*, Elizabeth Elliot tells of a major decision that Jim had to make many years before the above incident. Jim's parents, along with others who knew him well, could not help questioning whether perhaps his ministry should be among the young people in the United States. His gift for Bible teaching and preaching was an unusual one, as his college student work, radio preaching and evangelistic meetings had demonstrated. They wrote to him about their feelings, and mentioned as well their own sense of loss at seeing him leave home permanently. Jim Elliot had to face the decision whether it was God's will for him to stay at home or go overseas.

Every believer should face this decision, and yet so few do. For many of us the idea of serving God overseas doesn't enter our thinking. On the other hand, some of us have determined to go overseas, but in doing so we have failed to accept that it is God who commissions and sends, not ourselves.

The decision — home or overseas — is not a 'once-for-all' decision. I know some who have deeply wanted to go overseas, but for one reason or another God has indicated the time was not right. If this is your situation then be encouraged: it is not the end of the story. Continue to trust God. If he wants you overseas he will resurrect the matter in his time.

How does God call people overseas? If you were to ask a lot of missionaries, very few would give the same reply. We are all different, and therefore God treats us as individuals. This is how it happened with us:

At Bible college I was reading Ronald Sider's very disturbing book, *Rich Christians in an Age of Hunger* and Patrick Johnstone's book *Operation World*. My eyes were opened to the incredible need overseas. Starvation, poverty and millions who do not know Jesus Christ. It was this need that initially headed us in the direction of cross-cultural evangelism. I agree with Brother Andrew when he writes, 'What is a call? A call is to know about a need. We should obey the Scriptures where Jesus himself, in John 4:35, instructed us to lift up our eyes unto the fields. In other words, get acquainted with the vastness of the need.

'Too many Christians say, "I have no call". They say, "God never called me". But I say that you have never heard the call, because God has called you. He has told you to get acquainted with the need in the world. We complain sometimes about the modern news media, newspapers and television, that throw all the needs of the world into our living rooms. Actually, they leave us without a single excuse for saying that we do not know about the need.'[4]

I agreed with my friends who argued that in so-called developed countries like New Zealand and Britain many suffer from poverty and many do not know Christ. The needs are the same but their magnitude is far greater in some Third World countries. There are thousands of Christian workers in New Zealand and Britain but very few in many other countries. We sensed that God was calling us to the place of greater need.

Cross-cultural missions began to burn within our hearts. I devoured every book on the subject I could get hold of. I wrote to missionary friends and mission organisations asking for their advice. I knew that this decision had to be an intelligent one, based not just on a subjective call but also upon objective facts about missions and the world I lived in. So I researched magazines, newsletters and books. Throughout this time God confirmed the direction in which we were heading.

Finally, during a personal prayer time I got the distinct impression that God was asking us to go overseas. I left my office with a definite peace that this was the next step for us. Many tested me on this, for they questioned whether it was right for us to leave a successful ministry in New Zealand, but the conviction remained. We then sought God to know where he would have us go.

The choice between home and overseas will be easier to make if you keep talking to God and other people. God doesn't want you to face it alone. He loves you and wants to reveal his will to you more than you want to receive it. He has also placed you in the family of God for the encouragement, support and guidance you will need from other believers.

10
What Is My Ministry?

One summer on my father's farm, I got a real taste of back-breaking work. Early starts and late evenings were the norm of the day. Thoughts of 'I can't go on' and 'I am not cut out for this' welled up inside me, but it was shearing time and the job had to be done.

As there were hundreds of sheep to be shorn, a shearing team was employed. Dad and his dogs rounded up the sheep and brought them to the yards; another worker sorted them into pens; the shearers then did their back-breaking work. After each sheep was shorn, the floor was quickly swept by my younger brother, and it was my job to pick up the fleece and throw it onto the sorting table. From there it went into the bale and two strong men pressed it by hand, so it would then be ready to be taken to the wool auction.

In all there were about eight of us doing quite different jobs, but all of us belonged to the team and we all had one purpose in mind — the shearing of all the sheep. Many of us are in God's team of workers and have one purpose in mind — to extend his kingdom worldwide; but it is too general to talk simply about workers. We are all workers, but we differ in the particular job each of us has to do. Some are helpers, others teachers or preachers, others may be communication experts or technicians, and so on. How do I know what specific job God wants me to do? Do I spend many agonizing hours in prayer to show God how serious I am? Do I fast until the answer comes?

Prayer and fasting are beneficial, but there is another way of discovering his will which I think has too often been neglected, and that is to discover the gifts that God has graciously given us. This can be a real key to knowing his will for our lives. Peter Wagner brings this out in his excellent book *Know Your Spiritual Gifts.* We have all received at least one gift (1 Pet. 4:10; 1 Cor. 12:7) and these gifts are signposts to God's will (Rom. 12:1-8). For example, my mother-in-law has a gift of administration, and at this moment is a part-time administrator in her local church. Her gifts helped her to discover God's will.

If you do not know your gift, here are five practical ways that Peter Wagner gives, to help you discover them:

1.   Explore the possibilities. Get to know everything there is about spiritual gifts. Read the Bible and other books, ask others, observe others.
2.   Experiment with as many as you can. For example, you will never know if you are good at teaching unless you try it.
3.   Examine your feelings. What do you really enjoy doing? I personally get a lot of satisfaction out of doing research and communicating. It is in these two areas that I think God has gifted me.
4.   Evaluate your effectiveness. Gifts are given to benefit others. For instance, I would doubt that a person has a gift in administration when all he does continually turns into chaos and confusion, and utterly frustrates others.
5.   Expect confirmation from others [1]. Others usually know us better than we know ourselves.

Gifts and the world Christian at home

Trying to extend God's kingdom through mere self-effort is a waste of time. The Bible tells us that the flesh (self-effort) profits nothing. A Christian requires spiritual gifts to effectively implement Jesus' commission to 'go and make disciples of all nations' (Matt. 28:19). Knowing our gifts and using them gets us involved in world outreach. Let me illustrate this from the lives of some friends of mine.

Murray and Marti have real gifts in giving, and because of their persistent and generous giving, some workers overseas have the means to carry on with their vital work. Don is the Missionary Chairman in his church. God has given him gifts in leadership and faith. These gifts enable him to discern where God wants the church to be involved in missionary outreach and support.

Ruth, a mother of two, has a gift of encouragement. She writes up to twenty letters a week to overseas workers. I used to receive her letters while I was in training, and they were very encouraging. Ken has a gift of helping others. He would like to use his gifts to assist missionaries with their travel and baggage arrangements. You can be very specific and practical when it comes to using your gifts. Basil has a ministry in intercession. He spends many hours praying for the Lord's work overseas.

We all have an obligation to pray, give and be involved in world outreach, whether we have certain gifts or not. Beyond that we can all have our special areas of involvement, due to our gifts. Get to know your gift(s) and you get to know where you can make a real contribution in God's world today.

Gifts and the overseas candidate

The same applies to the person going overseas. His gifts are a good indicator of the kind of ministry he is to have. If he is a gifted evangelist at home, then more than likely he will be an effective evangelist overseas. The person and the gift don't change, simply the geographical location.

The missionary gift

Not all gifts are mentioned specifically as such in Scripture. Music is a case in point and another is the gift of being a missionary. Peter Wagner describes this gift as 'The special ability God gives to some members of the Body of Christ to minister whatever other gifts they have in a second culture.'[2]

He goes on to say that people who have this gift usually:
1. Enjoy coming into contact with other cultures.
2. Enjoy the challenge of living in another culture while cutting ties with their first culture on a long-term basis.
3. Recover rapidly from culture shock.
4. Eventually become immune to the new bugs in the food and drink of another people.
5. Learn the language rapidly.
6. Feel at home with the people of a second culture.
7. Are accepted by the new culture as 'one of us'.[3]

However, because a person encounters a particular problem on the field, for example, finding it difficult to learn another language, or coming to terms with frog's leg soup, does not mean he hasn't got a missionary gift. The Apostle Paul was a missionary and he faced many difficulties. This gift does not make a person an instantly perfect missionary. It merely enables him to cope with, and indeed learn to live with some of the trials experienced in another country.

You don't have to go to another country to see whether you have this gift or not. You can find out in your own city, by spending time with some of the ethnic groups near you. An Australian girl at the college I attended told me her interest in missionary work began when she came into contact with some Arabs in Sydney. They soon became her friends, and it got to the stage where she was spending more time with them than anyone else. Through being with these Arabs she discovered she had the ability to relate cross-culturally.

Part 3
LET'S DO IT TOGETHER

11
Meeting Together

'D-Day in the Falklands. The British land, the Argentines strike back, and sparring turns into war.'[1] This was how *Time* magazine reported the worsening crisis between Britain and Argentina. Now imagine if, after April 2nd, when Argentine forces invaded and seized the Falklands, an SOS had gone throughout the United Kingdom: Margaret Thatcher, the Prime Minister of Britain, was on the lookout for one super-human 'war machine' who, all by himself, could give her the victory she so desperately wanted. Only one man was to be sent to the Falklands. He alone was to face the terror and might of the Exocet missiles and the Argentine forces. All responsibility for victory would lie on his shoulders. This sounds a ridiculous story, doesn't it?

Yet, some Christians today see themselves as super-human war machines of Christendom. They alone can defeat God's enemies. Let's be honest — sometimes we are tempted to think that God's hand is on us in a special way. That even God thinks we are different from 'normal' believers. That we have determination, sincerity, wisdom and the gifts of God's Spirit to be successful — where others have failed. We think we are God's answer to Christ's Church and mankind.

Moses had the same problem. For months he tried to lead 3,000,000 Israelites by himself. He alone had the word of God and so from dusk to dawn people lined up to see him. In the end it got too much for him and it took an interfering father-in-law, Jethro, to put things right. Jethro advised Moses that he needed other men to help, if he were to escape a heart attack and ensure that the Israelites reached the Promised Land.

Margaret Thatcher needed a whole army in the Falklands, and not just one hero, if she were to secure the British territory. Our ministry, too, will suffer if we try and go it alone. Moses needed others to achieve his objectives. If we, as world Christians, want to make advances into enemy territory, we must unite and fight together. A fellowship of disciples can do the work of the kingdom far more effectively than a single disciple operating by himself.

We need to gather together the people in our church who have a concern for the world. Of course, we need the permission and blessing of the pastor. We may call it a Missionary Committee, a World Watch Group or whatever. If there is already such a group in your church, then make yourself available to help out in some way. If not, and you are wondering who should belong to it, look for born-again disciples who could make a real contribution to such a group; those, for example, with gifts in faith, administration, intercession, teaching, giving and so on. It would be a great advantage to have representatives from all departments of the church. To give it a cross-cultural flavour try to recruit people from different backgrounds and ethnic origins. There is no harm in recruiting young Christians also, as they will provide some necessary enthusiasm.

Try to run a group without a leader and you will soon end up with no group. Someone needs to administer and co-ordinate the operations of the group. In time the right leader will emerge. Look out for a person who has a proven interest in missions; is either an official or unofficial elder in the church; is respected; is capable of administrating a committee and can relegate and delegate to others.

A word to those who already have such a group, and a missionary chairperson: He needs to be encouraged. If finances allow it send your chairperson to an important missionary conference or let him buy some missionary books on the church account. This will help him to be more aware of worldwide missionary needs, and will probably also encourage him in his job. If you want your chairperson to do a good job, be careful not to get him involved in any other church responsibilities. If yours is a big church with ministry teams of up to six or more paid workers, have you considered employing your missionary chairperson part-time or even full-time? I know a number of big churches which have done this successfully.

Once the group and leader have been established some of their responsibilities must be seen to be an integral part of the church; to be giving a constant missionary input into the church; to direct the financial and prayer support and to look for, interview and nurture prospective candidates for overseas work.

In the following chapters we will look at how we can more effectively research missions, give to missions, pray for missionaries and missions, what we can do as families, and how we can reach foreigners in our own cities for Christ. And the most exciting thing is this: all of these essential ministries can be done in groups. We don't have to be lone-rangers in world outreach.

12
Praying Together

A sad story is told of a missionary who went to the Far East. He was a young man who, with his wife and three children, embarked on what they thought would be a real adventure for God. Everything seemed to be going so well. Before they left, their home church gave them full assurance that it would support them financially and fervently pray for them. They didn't want to disappoint such a supportive church, so when they were out on the mission field they regularly sent back tapes and letters informing the church of their progress and prayer needs. Unbeknown to them however, only one person was interested in keeping up with their progress.

The couple's great adventure was turning into a great disaster. The husband had a difficult and frustrating time learning the language. There was great opposition from the government and other non-Christian forces in the country. Then tragically at only 26 years of age his wife contracted Blackwater fever. She lived only a short time, leaving him with three young children.

With his first term of service completed he returned

home. Knowing that there would be a mid-week prayer meeting at his church he went to it late and sat in the back pew. They prayed for the Sunday School picnic, the new building programme and the women's coming trip to a regional conference. After the benediction, which signalled the end of the meeting, he sat in his pew amazed and stunned. There was no mention of missionaries and no prayer for the lost overseas.

As the pastor finally approached him, the returned missionary suddenly cried out, 'Now I understand. This is the reason'. Not knowing what on earth he was speaking about the pastor replied, 'What do you mean?' 'Those years on the field. The difficulties. The pain. The lack of results. This is the reason.'[1]

According to the Scriptures, not praying for others is a sin: 'As for me, far be it from me that I should sin against the Lord by failing to pray for you' (1 Sam. 12:23). The tragic account of this missionary and his family illustrates why God calls it a sin.

The reason we don't get some things from God is that we don't ask him for them. If we want to receive from God we have a responsibility to ask: 'You want something but don't get it . . . You do not have, because you do not ask God' (James 4:2). Many of us would dearly love to see a multitude of unbelievers come into the kingdom through our ministries. Asking is the key. When we pray for the salvation of the lost our miracle-working God brings some into the saving knowledge of Jesus Christ. Unfortunately, the reverse is also true: through not praying for the lost we can impede God's saving acts throughout this world. I am not suggesting that prayer is the only means to secure the salvation of the lost, but in God's scheme of things it is vital.

Paul Billheimer, who in his eighties wrote the excellent book *Destined for the Throne*, which has subsequently become a best-seller, has this to say, 'No soul can be saved apart from intercession, and every soul who is saved, is saved because someone prayed who would not give him up to Satan. Therefore, a holy church, by her intercession or lack of it, holds the power of life or death over the souls of men.'(2)

The Bible teaches about God's sovereignty and choice, but it also teaches that we can prevent things from happening because we fail to pray. The message is loud and clear. If we move out into this world through our prayers, we can accomplish much overseas. From the room in which we pray we can be shaping the ultimate destiny of peoples and countries.

Evan Davies, the Principal of the Bible college I attended, tells of the time he was suddenly awakened from his sleep one night. He had an overwhelming burden to pray for Indonesia. So he prayed then and there. On the radio, the next day, it was reported that an attempted Communist takeover of Indonesia had failed. The country thus remained open to the gospel and overseas missionaries. Evan later found out that God had also placed this burden of prayer for Indonesia on many others. A nation's course was affected by an ordinary man's prayer, thousands of miles away in the smallest state of Australia.

It's no wonder that some of the more spiritually perceptive people have coined the following phrases:

* Whoever prays most, helps most.
* The results of foreign missions will be a hundredfold greater when the church is what she ought to be in the matter of prayer.
* God himself works through men and men work with God through prayer.
* God does nothing but in answer to prayer.
* Prayer is striking the winning blow, service is gathering up the results.
* The things we enjoy most can be found the hardest to do.

Making time for prayer and then attempting to actually pray can be a real battle. It seems as though every time we should pray excuses and diversions abound. We need more sleep; or just that little bit longer in the shower. Then there is that very good television programme tonight; and I must spend more time with my friends. At times we will do anything to keep ourselves from prayer. And yet, when we finally do make it, we enjoy praying and kick ourselves for not doing it more often.

Having a struggling prayer life does not mean we are spiritual wash-outs. If prayer is a real battle then let's be practical about it. Decide on a definite time when you are at your best to pray. Find a place where you will not be interrupted. Then stick to this time and place. If you tend to fall asleep while praying, stand up and walk around. If you fall asleep while standing up, you will wake up in no time! If wandering thoughts are a problem, pray out loud. Praying for thirty minutes, an hour or even three hours will be no problem if we attempt these three simple steps.

Prayer was never intended to be only a solitary activity. Remember the account of Peter in Acts 12, where he was arrested and imprisoned? Upon hearing this, did the believers all rush off to their respective homes to pray alone? No, they got together in someone's house and prayed for Peter. I believe the early churches intercessory prayer life was effective, because it was a frequent group activity.

A missionary prayer group that my wife Robyn and I were once invited to would serve as a good model for any world outreach meeting. When we got there the room was packed and half of them were young people. They began with a time of worship. Right from the outset God was put at the centre of things. A time of personal sharing followed. Then they got down to the business of prayer. After praying for the needs of the people in the group they prayed for their churches. The leader of the group then asked for missionary prayer items. With that — newsletters, missionary letters and general world concerns came to the fore. These were read, discussed and prayed about. The hour they spent together culminated in a time of singing and thanksgiving. There was a conviction that God had heard the many prayers and was going to answer them. Finally, supper was served. The possibilities for such a group are endless. For example:

1. A group can concentrate on a certain region, country or people — such as France, the Middle East or Muslims.
2. Give time for educating the group. Look at Hinduism, the history of Christianity in Central America, what God is currently doing in Spain, etc.
3. Be a goal-orientated group. Believe that God will increase your group by the end of the year so that you can split it and begin a second. Start a fund-raising project, trusting God to provide a certain amount by a certain date.
4. Spend a weekend together, specifically for fellowship and prayer.
5. If a network of groups is operating, let the leaders meet together once a month to co-ordinate planning, teaching and to encourage each other.

I have already illustrated how our prayers can change a nation. But to pray intelligently we need information on the countries we want to pray for. *Operation World* by Patrick Johnstone, and other books mentioned in the booklist, will be of immense help.

'God bless . . .' prayers are prayed by us all. They mean we have run out of things to say. It is difficult to pray for someone for more than five minutes. If the missionary was prayed for yesterday what more can we pray for him today? To help us overcome this, Stewart Dinnen, a world authority on missions, compiled these twenty pointers:

1. Know the facts, understand their situation.
2. Concentrate, get to know the missionaries God wants you to pray for.

3. Know about their mission, its principles, methods and goals.

4. Understand the true nature of their work; is he a doctor, a dentist, administrator or evangelist? Pray accordingly.

5. Recognise the factors that oppose their ministry; alien culture, hostile people, tension, physical discomfort.

6. Pray that the missionary will know his [position of] authority over Satan.

7. Pray for the missionary's personal walk with the Lord.

8. Pray for the missionary's physical well-being, health, etc.

9. Pray for the missionary's mental well-being; language learning, making decisions in a foreign culture, personal reading, etc.

10. Pray for the missionary's family; children often suffer from sickness and the wife from loneliness and depression.

11. Pray for the missionary's attitude to other missionaries.

12. Pray for the missionary's attitude to the lost.

13. Pray for the missionary's relationships with the national Christians, that he will be humble and a servant.

14. Pray for a strong national church in the missionary's region.

15. Pray for the strengthening of the missionary's team where it is needed; more workers, resource aids, etc.

16. Pray with faith; God wants us to pray in line with his purposes. Prayer is co-operating with him in his strategy.

17. Pray consistently and persistently (Luke 11:1-10).

18. Praise God for the answers, and praise him also by faith — before they come.

19. Write away for special prayer points.

20. Prove the sincerity of your prayers by helping his mission organization back home in any way you can.[3]

Charles Spurgeon, the famous Baptist minister of years past, tells of the time when someone wanted to see him while he was busy in prayer. 'He was very great and important, and so the maid came to say that someone desired to see me. I bade her say that it was my rule to see no one at that time. Then he was more impressive and important still, and he said, "Tell Mr Spurgeon that a servant of the Lord Jesus Christ desires to see him immediately". The frightened servant brought the message; but the sender gained little by it, for my answer was, "Tell him I am busy with his Master, and cannot see servants now."'[(4)]

We watch a TV drama intensely. Frustration boils up within us when we are interrupted by commercials or, after a busy day at work, we love to sit down with the family and enjoy the evening meal together – uninterrupted. So like Spurgeon, when it comes to prayer, let nothing interfere with this most important and world changing exercise.

13
Thinking Together

One day I participated in a very foolish prank with a friend. His parents had gone into town and we were left alone on the farm. We decided to empty the chicken trough and replace the water with alcohol. You can imagine the outcome! Hens were running in all directions, crashing into one another and making a frightful noise!

However, even from this bizarre incident a very important lesson can be learnt. Obviously the alcohol inside the hens caused them to behave in a very peculiar fashion. It's the same with us. What we fill our hearts and minds with, determines how we act and what we do. The way we think will determine the way we live.

The American author Tim LaHaye has written a book entitled *The Battle for the Mind*. There are many forces today endeavouring to take control of our minds. If we want to be effective world Christians then it's paramount that we saturate our minds with God's thoughts, found in the Bible.

If we want the Bible to work in our lives then we need to constantly read it. And that takes time. This question was asked in a devotional life survey — 'What is the one greatest obstacle you struggle with in your devotional life?' The respondents included the following:[1]

Time	34%
Distractions	9%
Consistency	7%
Discipline	6%

Time is by far the greatest problem. Richard J. Foster, in his book *Celebration of Discipline*, says, 'In contemporary society our Adversary majors in three things: noise, hurry and crowds. If he can keep us engaged in "muchness" and "manyness", he will rest satisfied. Psychiatrist C.G. Jung once remarked, "Hurry is not of the devil; it is the devil." We live in an "activity" orientated society. So many demands are made upon our time. We constantly hear ourselves and others complain that there is rarely enough time to do all that we want, and Bible reading is so often one of the first things to fall by the wayside. What a tragedy.'[2]

It is to our shame that many non-Christians find the time to daily discipline themselves in TM and yoga exercises. TM and the like are spiritually misleading, but if their adherents can devote an hour a day to such activities, is it too much to expect and challenge the Christian disciple to take seriously the many instructions in the scriptures to be still before God and to meditate upon his word? The Bible is the stuff that the world Christian is made of.

Bible reading should not just be a solitary exercise for the world Christian. Public devotions are just as important. World Christians need to glean together the gems from God's word. There is much we can learn from each other. The Early Church met together in houses to read and study the Old Testament as well as the New Testament letters. These were largely written to groups of people, not individuals. (The pronoun 'you' occurred in the plural form rather than singular). I believe we miss a lot of God's truths because we read alone.

How to create a world Christian Bible study

Focus your Bible study on these basic questions:[3]

1. What does it say? Investigate the passage with: what? where? when? how? why? And then: How do my/our various discoveries relate to one another?

2. What does it mean? What is God trying to say through this passage? What are its implications for other biblical truths? What warnings does he give? What promises? What principles for daily living? What should be the impact of the passage on God's people anywhere?

3. What does it mean to me/us? Apply the passage in a very personal way: What does it mean to my/our walk with the Lord? To my/our dreams? My/our needs? lifestyle? daily responsibilities? priorities? relationships to other people? churches and families?

4. What does it mean to us as world Christians? What aspects of our world vision does it help us to build? Purpose? Possibilities? People? Part? How could it help equip us, train us, direct us and challenge us in the specific ways we are seeking to reach out in love right now? How could it help us give a world vision to someone else? What have we found here that we could share with another Christian to help them grow as a world Christian?

5. What does it mean to us as a team of world Christians? How does it stimulate, reinforce or reshape all we are trying to do together with Christ?

6. Use a coloured marker to highlight every verse that refers to God's concern for, evaluations of, intentions toward, actions toward, or involvement with the nations.

Global thinkers

Having a brainstorm over the Bible is one way of thinking together. A further and equally exciting way is to keep abreast with what is happening in the world. This will prove to be thought-provoking and stimulating. All at once you will have to be newshounds, researchers, bookworms, global politicians, world authorities, thinkers and strategists for God!

The Olympic Games are action-packed days of contest. Unfortunately, not many of us are able to attend them. So to learn how our champions have fared we eagerly await the sports news on radio or television. It's the same in the kingdom of God. We have our representatives out on the field. Their contest lasts many years and they're racing against the forces of darkness. It's their news we want.

During the Second World War people flocked to the papers and bulletin boards to learn how their forces had done in battle. As worldwide soldiers of Christ, we have a duty to keep up with what our Commander-in-Chief is doing on other battlefronts around the world. We need to know where his army is fighting, and what the campaigns are. To get this kind of information you have to go out and look for it. Such knowledge, however, will revolutionise your life. Andrew Murray, in *The Key to the Missionary Problem*, writes: 'Ignorance is the source of weakness in missionary effort. Know, and you will believe. Know, and you will pray. Know, and you will help in the front rank.'[4]

For a number of years I was ignorant of God's worldwide concern. I didn't think that mission was where the action was, for someone who wanted to live an exciting Christian life. In my first year at Missionary Training College (and I didn't go there because of its missions emphasis) I loathed the missionary prayer times. I tried to pick arguments with the visiting missionaries, and I refused to read the mission books on our recommended reading list. Then it all changed. I read Patrick Johnstone's book *Operation World* and Ronald Sider's *Rich Christians in an Age of Hunger*. As I read these books, the world, as it really was, opened up before me.

I began to see the suffering, pain and spiritual bondage that was the lot of millions. Then I looked at myself. I enjoyed three good meals a day. When my Bible got slightly tattered it was very easy to go and buy another. When it got cold I could turn on a heater or light a fire. I had a roof over my head. I had so much and I was taking it all for granted. There were so many luxuries I could over-indulge in while all around me there were millions who were dying for lack of them. It just didn't seem right — and it wasn't. I knew then, that even though I was a small fish in a very big pond, I had to do something about it.

I was determined, from that moment on, not to be ignorant of the needs of other peoples in this world. I listened to missionaries; I noted other countries' prayer needs. I fervently prayed for the overseas workers that were mentioned on the next Wednesday afternoon. I swallowed every crumb of information I could get. As I did, my affair with the world grew deeper and deeper. 'Know, and you will believe. Know, and you will pray. Know, and you will help in the front rank'. When we begin to think world outreach, we will begin to live it.

Fact finding

Why not adopt a missionary? There is no better way to get involved in world outreach than by writing to someone in the thick of it. Write to missionaries from your own city or state. Failing that, someone from your own country. If you don't know of one, just ask around. Your church is bound to have contact with at least one missionary, and mission societies usually list their own overseas workers.

Write to the missionary as you would a friend. Be natural. Nothing turns a person off more than a super-spiritual letter. Tell them what is happening at home, send newspaper clippings, enclose your church newsletter, and remember cards for birthdays, anniversaries and Christmas Day. Be personal and develop an intimate relationship through your letters. And don't forget your sense of humour!

You take the initiative and write the first letter. Even if the missionary doesn't reply, send another letter. He or she could have been too busy. Try and write once a fortnight, or once a month. Remember to send your letter off as soon as you have written it. That way you will not lose it, or forget about it.

God chose to use letters (epistles) to speak to us, and thousands have enjoyed his love-letters in the Bible. We all love to receive letters. Be assured — the lonely missionary will appreciate your letters.

Further information can be gained through watching television. There are usually some good 'current affairs' programmes, and documentaries on different countries. At the beginning of the week, mark them out and plan to watch them. Watch the evening news every day. Television provides up to date information; let's make use of it. Finally, read newspapers, and magazines such as *Time* or *Newsweek*. And don't skip the international pages. *The National Geographic* and encyclopedias also contain a wealth of information.

Magazines, books, study courses, missionary organisations, and letters from overseas workers are some of the key channels to obtain the knowledge we need. For this reason I have included some examples of source material in the Further Information at the end of this book that will help you on the way. As you research and discover, share your findings with others. In search of a major breakthrough, scientists will often pool their knowledge. As we pool our knowledge, God can begin to do his miraculous work in our lives, our churches and in our world.

14
Giving Together

A man complained to his pastor, 'It's getting to be just one continuous give, give, give.'

Said the pastor, 'You have just given one of the best descriptions of Christianity that I've ever heard!'[1]

Billy Graham endorses the pastor's reply by saying, 'The key word of the selfish, unregenerate person is – get. The key word of the dedicated Christian should be – give.'[2]

Christians tend to fall into two camps when it comes to money. First, there are those who see it as unalterable evil. They would agree with the words of the pop song:

'money – root of all evil / money – root of all evil
take it away / take it away / take it away'

Their line would be similar to that of Aristotle or Karl Marx. If you abolished all money then you would eradicate all the social injustices and sin.

The second camp goes to the other extreme. Money becomes one of the prime reasons for living. It is to be desired and obtained at all costs. To ascertain how successful a person is, one merely finds out what his assets and bank balance are.

Both of these schools of thought are wrong. Scripture does not call money either bad or good. God is concerned about our attitudes to money. It is these that are good or bad. It's the love of money, not money itself, that is the root of all evil.

'Get all you can, save all you can, and give all you can'. These are the three rules that guided John Wesley in the use of his money, and they just about sum it all up. It is biblical and legal to earn money, save money and give money away. The problems arise when we neglect one of these rules and live by the remaining two: If we don't earn money it is impossible to save it and give some away. This does not apply to those who are called to completely trust God for their needs. If we earn money and save it, but don't give any away, we're living extremely selfish lives that are contrary to God's word. If we give all our money away, without saving any, when that rainy day does come we might find ourselves in some trouble. To look after ourselves and our families, we must put some money away. Saving shows foresight, independence and self-denial. We can store in the sense of saving without hoarding.

Hoarding and covetousness are the two diseases that cripple missionary giving. We are told: 'Do not store up for yourselves treasures on earth' (Matt. 6:19), and 'For everything in the world – the cravings of sinful man, the lust of his eyes and the boasting of what he has and does – comes not from the Father but from the world' (1 John 2:16). Wanting too much money can ruin a Christian's ministry. In the Bible we note how for money Achan brought defeat on the armies of Israel and death on himself. For money Balaam tried to curse God's people. For money Gehazi lied to Naaman and Elisha, and became a leper. For money Ananias and Sapphira became the first hypocrites in the Early Church and subsequently lost their lives. For money Judas sold Christ and was ruined eternally.

Money is only a means, and not an end in itself. The Apostle Paul encourages us to be content with what we have got – rather than covet what we do not have. How do we get all we can without becoming covetous? The answer lies in giving all we can. The Sea of Galilee receives and gives water. It therefore remains healthy. The Dead Sea, however, receives water but never gives out any. The water is unhealthy and cannot support life. It is better to receive and give. In receiving alone we will not be able to support ourselves or anyone else.

Here are seven biblical words on giving to guide us[3]

1. *Cheerfully:* When the plate for missions comes around quietly say 'Hallelujah'. We are to give gladly, willingly, eagerly.

2. *Generously:* Our generosity is not seen in the size of our gifts but in the sacrifice that is involved.

3. *Secretly:* 'Not to let our right hand know what our left hand is doing'. We mustn't brag (remind ourselves and others) about our giving.

4. *Proportionately:* 'Give as the Lord has prospered us'. When more money comes in — give more.

5. *Regularly:* Weekly, or however often you receive your income.

6. *Widely:* Not just to our church, but also to the lost and the poor.

7. *Lovingly:* When we give, let it not be just a mechanical move of the hand from the pocket to the plate. As we give, let it be from the heart, as though we were giving ourselves.

During the Second World War people adopted a wartime lifestyle. They gave what they could to the war effort. As the war progressed they even gave out of their poverty – so their forces could remain fighting fit. Sacrifice was the norm. Christians are also in a war; Satan is the enemy seeking to destroy peoples and nations. The war is over people. The tragedy is that instead of adopting a wartime lifestyle the Church has chosen a peacetime lifestyle. Spending money on ourselves, interests, pleasures and wants is the norm, and because of this our forces overseas are having to go without many necessities. In places we are losing the war and millions have been lost to Satan.

Our Commander, the Lord of Hosts, commands us to suffer hardship (2 Tim. 2: 2,3) as good soldiers. That may mean going without, so that more money can be sent to those who really need it. Adopting a wartime lifestyle will mean less money for the world Christian. Those who are reasonably well off may need to adopt certain guidelines that will release more money in no time for world outreach:

1. Distinguish between necessities and luxuries. Reject any desire to chase the latter.

2. Expenditure for the purpose of status, pride, staying in fashion and 'keeping up with the Joneses' is wrong.

3. Distinguish between expenditure to develop one's particular creative gifts and legitimate hobbies, and a general demand for all the cultural items, recreational equipment and popular hobbies that the successful of our class or nation enjoy.

4. Distinguish between occasional celebration and normal day-to-day routine. Most of us overeat every day, and that is a sin.

5. There is no necessary connection between what we earn and what we spend on ourselves. We should not buy things just because we can afford them.

6. Start to move toward a lifestyle that could be sustained over a long period of time if it were shared by everyone in the world.[4]

There will always be people and missions who will appreciate our monetary support. As this happens in the world, it can also sadly happen in the kingdom of God. We can be persuaded and subtly coerced into giving our money to those who don't need it. I suggest the following cautions to help prevent us from making this mistake.

Firstly, we can easily be swayed by the 'personality' missionaries. They have a good story to tell and have the charismatic personality to tell it. To them we give a lot, but to the overseas worker who looks as though he has come out of the fifties, who speaks funny and is a bit shy, we give very little. In giving, it's not looks and charm that should persuade us, but rather how strategic his work is to the kingdom. We are not called to give prizes to the best personality, but to give where God is directing.

Secondly, we can easily be swayed by the 'results' syndrome. Joe Blow returns from the field. He tells amazing stories. He has statistics to prove it all. So out comes our money. His venture is successful so why not get behind it. Another missionary tells of only a few converts in his ministry. And that after twenty years! Only God can see all the factors behind these two very different stories. But to him both are important ministries, and it may be the latter who needs real support and encouragement.

Thirdly, we can easily be swayed by the 'need' syndrome. Marjorie Collins, author of many missionary books, gives us this advice: 'Don't support an orphan because you feel sorry for him. Don't support a cause just because your pastor thinks you should. Don't support a project because it sounds exciting. Support something you can give to wholeheartedly, as unto the Lord.'[5]

It is important to note the need, but also to recognise that the need by itself may not mean God is calling you to fill it.

Fourthly, don't get swayed by every 'Christian' organisation. Unfortunately, there are some questionable groups which operate as evangelical missions. They make appeals and accumulate funds but only for their own gain. Investigate any group or person before you decide to give. Check with a trusted pastor or Christian leader for his evaluation of the organisation. Ask for the statement of faith to which the organisation adheres. Beware of extravagant, unrealistic claims about results. If necessary and possible, ask for the missionary organisation's financial statement so that you can see a breakdown of their income and expenses. Seek to determine what proportion of money is going to meet the objectives of the mission. Be wary if the mission seems insulted by your request.

Faith promise giving

1972 was the turning point for Spreydon Baptist Church. That year they held a missionary convention. The aim was to stimulate missionary concern and giving in the church. In 1973 they introduced the faith promise plan. They had hoped that £1,200 would be promised for the coming year's missionary outreach. Instead, £4,400 was promised. In 1981, £28,800 was promised and the following year £48,000. A revolution in missionary giving had taken place in that church. The key was the faith promise plan.

Don McKenzie, their missionary chairman, explains the faith promise plan:

'The key to faith promise giving is that you ask God how much he wants you to give to the worldwide spread of the gospel . . . over and above what you give to your local church work.

You make a faith promise for a weekly amount, trusting that if God has impressed this amount on your heart, then he will supply it to you.

If the money is not available some weeks, then you are under no obligation to give. It is a faith promise offering, not a pledge. If some weeks the Lord enables you to give over what you initially thought possible, then praise God for it.

In this way we are helping to fulfill the Great Commission. Most missionaries have to live by this approach to financial giving, trusting in some way that money will become available for their work.[6]

Why is it so successful?

It is successful because faith is put to work, and faith pleases God. Each person has to go to God for the amount, and gives out of his obedience to his Lord.

Secondly, everyone can be involved – the young person on the minimum wage; the elderly on their pensions; the rich and the poor; students and workers.

It encourages united effort. The church pulls together to

make world outreach viable financially. And because there is an annual total, the missionary committee knows the amount it has to budget for.

It exposes the Christian to a life of faith. He gets a taste of seeing God answer his specific prayer. The Christian also enters into systematic, disciplined giving. He becomes a part of world outreach.

Finally, the missionary on the other end also benefits. He now has a fair idea of what he will get over the following year. The missionary is also comforted by the fact that each week he knows people are remembering him as they contribute to his efforts in world outreach.

Here is a testimony of a couple who explored the challenge of faith promise giving:

'My wife and I had heard how missionaries testify how they lived by faith. How God had supplied their needs, and as a result their own faith had grown. We asked ourselves whether we at home could also depend upon God to meet our needs. Faith promise gave us the answer to our question. We wanted to get involved in this plan. So how much should we give? Should we decide on an amount or let God reveal it to us? We decided to allow God to rule. We took the situation to him in prayer.

The Sunday in which we were to make our promise came. However, no amount had been made clear to us. Before we went to church we both prayed about it again. Still there was no conviction. To be honest though, I had an amount in my mind over the previous week. As I waited for my wife to get ready, a feeling came over me to double the amount that I had on my mind. This was really an absurd amount, I felt, as it was more than what we could afford. Later my wife asked me what amount had been revealed to me. I was too embarrassed to say, but when I finally admitted it, she had exactly the same amount.

By giving this amount to faith promise, it has meant that we must now live by faith. All that we have is now committed to him. If any of those unexpected expenses come, we have to trust God for his supply. We have nothing to meet that expense. There have been two such occasions when this has happened and each time God met us in a wonderful way. This, to us, is what living is all about. We have committed all to him. He has proved faithful to us. We thank and praise God for the challenge of faith promise giving. It's a new dimension of living.'

Before I came to the church that I am now pastoring they tried to implement the same plan and no-one would agree to it. Apparently it wasn't accepted because it wasn't adequately explained. This is the first key to implementing such a plan. Explain what you mean by the faith promise scheme. (You may have to do this three or four times.) If you have home groups perhaps go to each and explain the plan and allow plenty of time for questions. A seminar for the whole church would be another way of getting everyone together to explain it.

Firstly, explain the danger of emotionalism. People can give or promise out of emotionalism and not faith. As a result unrealistic amounts can be promised. People need to be aware that it is God who determines the amount, not their spirituality or emotions. Some can over-spiritualise the whole affair. They wait for God to give them a dream or for writing on the wall. All that is required is simple childlike faith. Believe that God will reveal the amount in his way and in his time.

Secondly, faith promise does not change God's priorities for the family. God would rather see a family have what it needs than go without necessities because either parent is adamant about giving hundreds of pounds. Many of us are eager to serve God, but we must couple our zeal with wisdom.

Thirdly, it is called faith promise, but faith has many servants that make it work. God may ask us to live a simpler lifestyle to see the promised amount realised. This is not taking the faith element away, but it would be ridiculous if Joe was intending to promise thirty pounds a week when he was also spending twenty pounds on records and car parts for his latest hot rod.

Fourthly, faith promise does not absolve a person or church from other commitments to world outreach. Prayer support is still vital. Training and sending prospective workers is still a must. Mission organisations still need practical support. It is but one part of a whole. Let's be balanced. To be honest, giving money does not require all that much effort. In one sense it is the easiest form of giving.

Its implementation

Once people understand the philosophy of faith promise giving, you can ask your new 'converts' to this plan to go and put their faith into practice. Each member is given a slip of paper outlining that they now have to come up with the sum that God is wanting them to believe him for.

XYZ Church
Missionary Convention
Faith Promise Amount

I hereby promise, before God, to trust him for

£ . . . . to give weekly to our church's

ongoing missionary programme.

Note that on this sheet the faith promise money is given weekly. This to my mind is best because it keeps people's minds on missions continually. You may however, want to do it fortnightly or monthly. Whatever works for you.

It is best that all the slips are handed in on one Sunday. Before the end of the service the total promised amount can be read out. It can be a high point in the church's life and service. An ideal context in which to implement and conclude the faith promise scheme is a special missionary convention. The faith promise total can be renewed, and will hopefully be higher at the next convention.

Distribution of money

For the missionaries' sake it is better that the cheques are sent out on the same date every month. This helps the missionary to budget accordingly. It can be extremely difficult to decide how much each missionary should receive. Should they all get the same? Or do some need more than others? When making these decisions, take into account the standards of living in each country. For example, the cost of living in Chile may be far higher than for a missionary in India. The Chilean worker may have to spend all his money on food and rent, but the worker in India, if receiving the same amount, may still have X amount of pounds left over after buying food and paying the rent.

The missionary needs support. But so does the mission society he represents. If we don't support the society, the missionary may still get to the field, but the mission will not be able to supply him with sufficient equipment to do the job effectively.

15
Evangelising Together

A friend of mine has a consuming passion to reach Russians for Jesus. He works as a micro-chemist in the local hospital. He has to do ordinary chores like mowing the lawns, paying the bills and cleaning the car, but what makes him unique is his compassion for Russians. He spends many hours learning their language. He writes to unknown believers in Russia, telling them of the love of Christ. As soon as a Russian ship arrives in port he reschedules his timetable so that he can go and meet the seamen and invite them out to dinner. You see, even though he is at home, he is still involved in world outreach.

We do not have to leave our home country to reach other ethnic groups: Asians, Africans, South and Latin Americans, Greeks and Italians. They can all be found in our neighbourhoods and cities. Some of them are here to work; others to study. We have our own cross-cultural mission field at home. God wants these people to come to know him, and he needs you and me to make that possible.

Many of the immigrants that we receive into our cities are extremely lonely. They have left behind their families, their familiar surroundings and their heritage. They are now all alone in the 'concrete jungle'. They want to be loved and made welcome. They desperately want to feel at home.

Paul E. Little was a marvellous communicator (he died in a tragic road accident while still quite young), and he had this to say about loneliness:

> 'One of the prominent symptoms of our times . . . is loneliness. More people are desperately lonely than ever before. Even the high rise buildings in our big cities are monuments to loneliness. There is an aching loneliness behind those doors for many people. I know of those, both in the city and in the suburb, who go to the large shopping centres simply for the opportunity to talk to somebody in the store. At least the checker will speak to them as they go out. Loneliness is one of the desperate problems of our age.'[1]

This is like the child who leaves home to go to school for the first time. For hours he is away from the comforting arms of his mother. All the faces in the classroom are unknown to him. He is frightened. He is lonely. Tears come to his eyes and he wants to go back home.

We must become personal friends with these lonely people. We should take the initiative to introduce ourselves. When we begin to talk to them about our city, and invite them over for a cup of coffee or tea, then they will begin to feel settled. And more importantly – their new friends will be Christians. Never fear that they will reject you. Remember, they want to be made welcome. They want to form meaningful relationships with the people of this new land. Usually they will be open to your friendly moves because they genuinely appreciate the fact that they have been allowed to enter your country.

Just ten feet away from where I am typing there is a six foot fence that separates me from my neighbours. This kind of barrier makes it almost impossible to talk with my neighbours. In our communication with foreigners there will be many barriers that have to be overcome. One key barrier is a conscious or unconscious attitude that we are superior to them, that we are right and they are wrong. This sort of communication barrier manifests itself when we patronise them. We communicate to them that we are doing them a favour. They resent our doing things *for* them rather than *with* them. They like to be looked upon as equals, not as a special class, or special case. Superficiality also ruins friendships. They want to get to know us and not just meet with us. For meaningful relationships to develop we will have to make some sacrifices. We mustn't treat them as potential converts, just souls to be won. They are human beings who need to be loved and respected, regardless of their religion or background.

Floyd McClung, a Director of Evangelism with Youth With A Mission, has devoted many years of his life to communicating with peoples from all backgrounds and nationalities. His message to all of us is 'friendship evangelism'. Jesus was a friend of sinners, so why can't we be? Often, however, we approach people with a charade of friendliness, only to cut them to pieces when the subject of Christianity is raised. We smile: 'How are you today? Are you having a good day? Fine. Let me share something with you . . .' And then POW! we slam them with the gospel.[2]

McClung advises us to 'evangelise because we care, and because we love people as ourselves'; 'people don't care how much we know until they know how much we care'. So how do we care? How do we develop a friendship with foreigners?

1. Put yourself in their shoes. Begin to imagine how you would feel, what you would think and how you would cope if you were suddenly in a new country. Coping with even the most basic things can be a nightmare!

2. Offer to take them to places of scenic, historic, cultural and professional interest.

3. After the friendship has begun to develop, you may feel free enough to suggest they come around to your place and

cook their national meal. To many this would be seen as a gesture of respect.

4. Include them in your regular activities as an individual or family. Our homes can become a home from home for them.

5. Share their activities and interests. Get to know what they like doing and participate if invited.

6. Help them out with the simple things of day-to-day living. Bus routes, currencies, names of foods, etc., will have to be explained to them.

7. Help them with their English, and while you are at it, get to know some phrases in their language.

Immigrants have broken loose from old associations, and initially are not hardened into new patterns of life. They are willing to make new friends and entertain new ideas. They are sometimes free from the social and religious bondages of their previous communities and are often receptive to all sorts of innovations, among which is the gospel. They are in a place of insecurity and therefore will reach out for something to stabilise them and raise their spirits.

So how do we communicate the gospel to the immigrants who are feeling this insecurity?

1. Pray that the Holy Spirit will give natural, not forced, opportunities to share with them what we have found in Christ.

2. We should never insist that they go to church with us, but simply invite them.

3. We need to realise that the words and concepts we use are totally foreign to them. Time must be spent in explanation and discussion.

4. Over a period of a year, such subjects as – 'What is God like?'; 'Who is Jesus Christ?'; 'Why did he die?'; 'The nature of man?'; 'What happened at the Resurrection?'; 'How does one become a Christian?' – could all be discussed.

5. We must answer the questions they ask. At times we will have to admit that we cannot answer them. We should

go home, research the answer and come back to them.

6. We must let them present their own points of view – even if it means listenening to a lecture on Buddhism for an hour or so!

7. At the appropriate time give them a New Testament in a modern version.

8. If there is no interest in Christianity shown, we must continue the friendship. By doing this we demonstrate our genuine interest in him as a person.

What could be better time than having a relaxing meal with friends? So why not invite them over for a night of fun? Always invite two or more at a time. They will be more at ease if a friend is present. Early on get to know and pronounce their names correctly. Because of their backgrounds, some may have certain dietary restrictions. Therefore do not force them or even urge them to eat things that may not appeal. Finally, be sure to invite them again.

16
Sharing Together

The missionary convention

The purpose of this is:

1. To inform the church what is happening in missions around the world.
2. To update the church members on whom they are supporting. This is also an opportunity to make the missionaries seem more personal, rather than just names.
3. To challenge the church to greater service and increased giving. An ideal opportunity, also, to recruit new candidates for world outreach.
4. To fix a goal for the coming year in faith promise giving.

Conditions for a successful convention

1. Plan it well: plan it in advance and publicise extensively and effectively.
2. Have it when maximum attendance is guaranteed. Public holidays and long weekends are usually unsuitable, as so many are away.

3. Obtain qualified speakers – not too many though.

4. Appoint a Convention Administrator. It is his job to ensure that everything runs according to schedule both in the build-up, and during the convention itself. This position should not be filled by the pastor; he has too many other things to think about.

5. Prayer is the key. Prayer – not organisation – will guarantee spiritual impact. Make full use of the church prayer meetings, and set up a special prayer group too.

The speakers

1. They must be able to speak clearly, simply and with impact. Nothing will kill a convention more than boring speakers!

2. They must be prepared to open themselves up and build relationships with the people.

3. They must be willing to be honest, frank, and transparent. Church folk want to see real people, not super-spiritual unreal missionaries.

4. They must have had some experience in cross-cultural work overseas; but the speakers should not just be limited to missionaries. There should be those who can bring messages on discipleship, the missionary calling, and so on. Speakers should be invited who can give an accurate overview of world mission today, and highlight the opportunities open to candidates for service.

Before speakers come to the convention, the pastor and Convention Administrator need to have been in contact with them and be fully informed of what the speaker intends to do and achieve. All misunderstandings and questions need to be dealt with during this time. Goals and emphases need to be clearly communicated by both the speakers. Don't be afraid to make it clear to the speakers that the church is running the convention; they are the guests.

The meetings

1. If the convention begins on a Tuesday and finishes the following Sunday, it is better that only a few of the week nights are taken up with *mass* meetings.

2. An ideal week night meeting place is the home. If a church has home groups, the speakers can visit them. The advantage is that the speakers can reach people who may not attend the *mass* meetings. Small groups promote better discussion, and they allow the speakers to move freely among the people. Testimonies, slides, interviews, questions, studies, etc., can take place in such a group.

3. The Sunday services are also a great opportunity. However, it is better to avoid prolonged descriptions of the missionaries' fields. Ten to fifteen minute interviews of the missionary, testimonies, and challenging sermons by gifted speakers usually go down best in a service.

The missionary on furlough

The traditional furlough lasts up to a year, and can be a rough time. The missionary is expected to carry out 'deputation' ministry, which often entails going over the same sermon and slides for months, in meeting after meeting! They may return to the field – suffering from mental fatigue and spiritual staleness – and be under financial pressure due to unrealistic giving.

Some get involved in this work because their mission societies expect them to; others do so because their congregations want them to. (It is sometimes the only way they can raise the money to go back to the field as well as solicit some prayer support.) For others it is an opportunity to present the challenge of the Great Commission.

Some form of deputation work is no doubt essential. There is no better way to communicate a world vision, than by a missionary who has recently returned from the mission field. However, we must be sensitive to the returning missionary and not expect him to be continually on the road. He needs time for fellowship in his home church so he can receive the necessary love and encouragement.

The scriptural furlough (read Acts 14: 26-28)

Paul and Barnabas returned to the church from which they were sent. They got the church together and told them about the wonderful things God had done through their ministry in other lands. Then, it says, they spent a long time with the disciples. They didn't travel all around the countryside giving sermons and appeals, but instead spent a considerable amount of time in fellowship with the people in their church. Maybe we need to remember this type of furlough for our returning workers.

What can we do as a church? Before the missionary returns home, we should find out from him whether he wants a house to move into. If so, we should do all we can to provide him with one. Does he want a part-time job? Has he got enough money to maintain himself on his furlough? Does his family need a holiday? All these questions and more should be asked, so we can assure the returning worker that we do indeed care for him and want the best for him while he is back with us. Upon his arrival we should take every step to include him and his family in the life of the church; fellowship being the main priority.

The pastors and leaders of the church should make it their aim to see that the missionary benefits from ministry while he is at home. This can be done by making books, tapes and study materials available to him. The returning worker needs to spend some time with the pastor, and he also needs the prayerful support of the whole church.

Speaking practically, he may need ordinary household items such as a toaster, an iron, furniture, jugs or food. He may also have returned home with the barest necessities in clothing.

Not only is this type of furlough scriptural, it is also economical for the mission societies, practical for the missionaries, illuminating for the church and really beneficial for all those concerned.

It all begins at home

The family is the most important unit in the world. It determines the strength, character and success of a society or country. Christian families determine the success of world outreach. World evangelisation begins with the family. When the family is disinterested, there is little fruit on the mission field. Each family unit can help reach the 3,000,000,000 who still haven't received Christ.

Responsibilities of the parents

1. To teach their children well. If parents want to see their children become mature Christians, they must be examples for their children to follow.

2. To give their children over to the Lord, as Abraham did with Isaac, Hannah with Samuel, and Manoahs's wife with Samson. They relinquished the ownership of their children, and gave God the right to do with them as he pleased. This is what Christian parents need to do, so that he can fulfill his good and acceptable purposes in their lives, and thus extend his kingdom.

3. To develop an awareness in missions. If the parents are active and verbal in their interest in missions and the world, the children will catch their enthusiasm.

4. To be willing to let their sons or daughters go overseas. Many Christian parents have applied different forms of emotional blackmail to try and keep their children near them. Parents must, in God's strength, cut the cord and let their children serve God where he wants them.

How to get children interested

1. Young children love to hear stories – why not missionary ones?

2. Young children love to colour in – why not pictures of foreign places and peoples?

3. Children and teenagers are intrigued by strange and

foreign objects. Why not take them to exhibitions and the local museum?

4. Watch TV programmes that focus on another country.

5. Quiz your children on their knowledge of the world. Make this a game – it can prove to be a lot of fun.

6. Ask your children to help you pray for other countries and workers. They will appreciate being asked, and their childlike faith is pleasing to God.

7. Encourage your children to have a pen-pal with a child of similar age overseas.

Involving the whole family

1. Don't have long, boring prayer times. God listens to short sentence-like prayers. Instead of forcing prayer on your children, guide them into it.

2. Don't be unreal. Have a genuine interest in world outreach, not a superficial one. Your children will see whether you are doing it to impress them, or because it is the right thing to do, or because you are doing it out of love and compassion for the lost and needy.

3. Don't force missions onto your children, instead guide them into it.

4. Don't communicate that the only way to be involved is through prayer and giving money. Be creative and use your imagination.

5. Don't try and do it all by yourself. Ask God for his help.

Getting others interested

'As iron sharpens iron, so one man sharpens another' (Prov. 27:17). People respond to people, and if others are to be drawn into world outreach, then we must be the ones to make that possible. We can do this in a variety of ways. Visiting speakers can come and take one Sunday service a month for a purely mission thrust. If you cannot obtain a visiting speaker, then use one of your own missionary-minded, gifted speakers. Use this service as an opportunity to interview your own members who are actively involved in various forms of outreach. Then pray for them.

Make sure that all educational departments in your church emphasise world outreach at least once a month in their programmes. This includes the youth group, Sunday school, adult classes, Bible study groups and home groups. Remember to be creative.

Audio-visuals, videos and films can be obtained from mission societies or film distributors. They can be shown in mid-week meetings, conventions, special Saturday night showings or even the Sunday service. The ideal place is the home group, when a time of discussion can take place after the showing.

A short skit or play in a service can be very effective in communicating a world vision. Music, and not simply choruses or hymns, is also effective. I have found that solos and duets are very effective as far as music is concerned.

Put up a missionary bulletin board. It should be placed where everyone can see it. Maps, posters, missionary newsletters, photos of overseas workers, general information and so on can all be placed on the board.

My church sends out a missionary newsletter. Not only should some information of world outreach be included in the weekly church newsletter, but special world outreach newsletters could be distributed once a month. Facts relating to the world situation, your own missionaries, and other prayer needs, as well as a few photos, can all go in the newsletter. For this to really take off the World Outreach Committee needs to find a talented person who has both the time and ability to put it together. The information in the newsletter needs to be up-to-date. For this to happen, a good correspondence network needs to be in operation. Remember to delegate.

World outreach dinners are very popular. This could be a cultural evening. Not only is it an ideal opportunity for fellowship, but it is also a time for people to discover more about the world they live in. This could be done once a quarter, or if possible, once a month. The evening could concentrate on a particular region, people or country. For example, a Chinese night would include a Chinese meal, Chinese dress, a Chinese visitor giving a short address on his country or a missionary from that land. Posters on China should decorate the walls, and if possible Chinese music played throughout the evening. There are many ways of doing this. Be creative.

Home groups are where the people are. A slot could be made available each week for the group to discover more about their involvement in the world, its needs and so on. Prayer for a particular church missionary or country could follow. The home group leader need not be the person who leads this.

Finally, there is the bookstall. Include books about the world on your bookstall: biographies, autobiographies, study materials, informative books and novels are just some of the many types of books that can be displayed. Set up a world outreach library. Advertise it by giving short book reviews in a service, study or home meeting. Pass a good book onto a friend.

Your pastor needs encouragement

The 'smiling parson' or a 'superstar'? Drinking cups of tea and eating cucumber sandwiches with the elderly folk are considered the responsibilities of the former; and the latter is expected to do everything and do it well. Thankfully, the Bible does not ask the pastor to be either of these: ' It was he who gave some to be apostles, some to be prophets, some to be evangelists, and some to be pastors and teachers, to prepare God's people for works of service, so that the body of Christ may be built up' (Eph. 4:11,12).

The pastor exists to train the members of his church to go out and do the work of the kingdom. The work of the kingdom is the making of disciples in all nations (Matthew 28:19). This should be his chief concern, yet sadly many pastors do not even have an interest in world outreach.

A number of reasons contribute to this: It could be that

their training does not emphasise world mission. Systematic theology, pastoral theology, Greek and Church history are all taught, but theological colleges seldom give training in how to plan and carry out a missions programme in the local church. In America, for example, only 6% of those schools that train pastors, demonstrate in their curriculum that a missions programme in the local church has any importance.[1] Our colleges and seminaries have produced a generation of pastors who have not been taught that missions is an important part of their local church.

Then, their ambitions do not allow for it. Some pastors are pulled in two directions: they realise the world needs to be reached but they are also rightly concerned about helping their church to grow. This latter concern can cause them to forget about God's worldwide kingdom. In time, they cannot see beyond their own corner, suburb and church. One of the greatest hindrances to world outreach is the 'entrenched pastor'.

Many churches expect their pastors to be the superman I mentioned before. They are expected to do everything. What results is the one man show, with the pastor running around trying to keep everyone happy and the whole operation moving. As a result he has not got the time to plan and implement a missions programme, or equip the saints.

The pastor is important

Sheep follow their shepherd. When a pastor moves away from world outreach, he leads his flock in the same direction, because they will follow him. It is well-known that the people will get excited about whatever enthuses the pastor. Pastors have a tremendous influence over their church members. Through this influence he can squash the vision for world outreach in others, thus robbing many of a chance to serve the Lord in helping others.

When a pastor tries to do everything himself, he robs

others of the opportunity to serve God and use their gifts. A person who is not serving in his own church will hardly be motivated to serve God elsewhere. Jesus' disciples began their ministry in their home town of Jerusalem, but finished it all over the world (Acts 1:8). Once a person gets a taste of ministry in his home church, he will soon want to reach the whole world for Christ. When a pastor robs his church of the opportunity to minister, he also robs God of potential world Christians.

Some pastors think that if they supported world outreach too strongly, their financial support and young people would be diverted away from their church to other parts of the world. Their fear of losing money and people cripples world outreach. They have failed to realise God's law of giving and receiving. When a church begins to give to the needy in the world, God sees to it that they receive what they need. Most of the churches today that are experiencing real church growth, also have an active missionary thrust. They are giving and God is supplying.

Becoming a world-thinking pastor requires the study of the Word. He needs to know how God sees the world; he needs to know the love of Christ for the world and have an understanding of how the local church can demonstrate this love. However, mere head knowledge or mental assent is not enough. Such truths need to explode in his heart, and only the ministry of the Holy Spirit can make this happen.

He needs to study the world situation. What are other countries like? How well off are we compared to other lands? Patrick Johnstone's book *Operation World* is ideal for this kind of study. An awareness of need is the first step towards some form of action. Time spent in prayer is always helpful. He needs to ask God to transform him into a world Christian. He needs to pray that his church will catch a vision for the world. And finally, time must be spent in prayer for the world.

Dialogue with other world Christians is essential. Whether they be church members, missionaries or mission society representatives. I am not just talking about planning or question-answer sessions, but times when the pastor and the world Christian can have meaningful fellowship on a deep and personal level.

Time and funds should be made available for the pastor to go and see a church that is already effectively fulfilling the Great Commission. The pastor should not rule out the possiblity of visiting the missionary field himself. I would be the first to admit that this is not possible for all pastors, but if the time and money is forthcoming he should grab the opportunity. An eye-witness account of the missionary field can give the pastor a passion for the world, as nothing else will.

What the pastor can do

Be more 'world' orientated in his preaching. If each pastor stressed the need to see the salvation of the lost overseas, the urgency of discovering God's will for one's life and the call to service, there would be a marked increase in interest in world outreach. What a pastor fills his members" minds with, determines to a large extent what they become and do.

The pastor should aim to release his members for the work of service. World outreach will never catch on unless this is done. He must let others discover the excitement that there is in serving God overseas. The pastor's role is to equip his members for the work of service. If a pastor is doing this, then he is providing a pool of workers for God to use in the extension of his kingdom. He can help initiate a World Outreach Committee in his church. If one already exists then he should maintain close links with it, especially with the chairperson.

The pastor could also ask a missionary to work in the church for a brief time prior to his leaving for work overseas. This way the pastor can have a real part to play in the preparation of the missionary, and the church also benefits from getting to know the missionary personally. A returning missionary will also need the pastor's help as he seeks to re-establish himself in his original cultural setting. The pastor can also write to those missionaries the church is supporting.

The pastor can assist and encourage the serious missionary candidate in his church, by communicating to him that he has his total support in what he is doing and by being available for counsel. Remember he is going out to the front lines of battle and so needs all the spiritual support he can get. The pastor should be prepared to pass on all he knows to the serious candidate. Finally, the pastor is able to build his mission programme around this missionary. There is no better way of generating a mission interest in the church than by involving their own missionary candidates.

What about the pastor going?

Michael Griffiths makes the following statement. 'It cannot escape the careful reader of the New Testament that those who were sent out as missionaries by those first century churches were themselves already experienced Christian workers.'[2] For example, Paul, Barnabas, Silas and Timothy (Acts 13 - 16). A pastor should never think that because he has been called to a local church in his own country, future work overseas is no longer an option. I have just heard of a man who has faithfully ministered in New Zealand for a number of years as a local pastor, but is now off to Papua New Guinea.

Generally, it is the Bible college graduate that we send over and not the trained and experienced pastor. We must send our most trained and experienced men over; we must send our best. They must be people whom we will miss. Only those who are making a contribution now, will make an impact overseas.

Pastor – be excited about your ministry

When I was a pastoral worker at Spreydon Baptist Church, I knew of many more young people who were eager to get into full-time service, whether it was at home or overseas. I have just read of a church in England, that over a period of five years saw over 150 of their congregation entering full-time missionary service or enter the ministry of the church at home. Why is it, that in some churches droves of young people are coming forward who want to get involved with full-time work; while in other churches you only get the odd one or two? I tend to think the pastor is a key factor.

You could tell without having to listen to him, that Murray Robertson, the senior pastor at Spreydon, was enthusiastic and excited about his job. He loved it, and he was obviously satisfied and fulfilled in it. Many of us tried to be like him, and wanted to follow in his footsteps. Not only this, he was also successful in what he was doing. Many were being converted, people were receiving healing and the church was growing with a 20+% annual rate. He communicated to the young people that full-time service could be extending, profitable and exciting.

If we as pastors want our young people to seriously consider full-time service, we had better prove to be effective and attractive examples. Through our words or actions we are either turning people off full-time service or attracting them to it.

Part 4
GOING OVERSEAS

17
Qualifications

The sons of Reuben and the sons of Gad begged Moses to let them settle down in Jazer and Gilead, rather than go across the Jordan. They had an exceedingly large number of livestock and 'this side of the Jordan' suited them nicely. In essence, they were saying to Moses, 'This land needs livestock and we have got the livestock; we should therefore stay'.

Many Christians have this same attitude. My country needs good pastors and teachers and I have the necessary 'gifts' in these areas. I am suited to my own culture and therefore I will not travel beyond this land.

Moses rebuked the Reubenites and Gadites. In their desire to stay 'on this side of the Jordan' they were leaving the responsibility of fighting God's enemies in the Promised Land to the other tribes. They were opting out of God's work and this had the effect of discouraging the other tribes. Because many of us have refused to go overseas, even when God has called us, we have left the spiritual war to a relatively small number. It is no wonder that they are discouraged at times. God is also grieved.

We may be suited to our own country and be exercising a dynamic and fruitful ministry, but that does not automatically mean God does not want us overseas. In God's scheme of things, a successful ministry in one's own country may only be preparation for an even greater ministry overseas.

Jesus had this to say, 'The harvest is plentiful but the workers are few. Ask the Lord of the harvest, therefore, to send out workers into his harvest field' (Matt. 9: 37,38). Jesus knew that there would always be a shortage of labourers. That is why he beseeches us to make this a real matter of prayer. We must always keep before us his desire to see workers move out into the world.

In many countries today the harvest is plentiful. Africa, Indonesia and South America are full of people who are ready for the gospel, but there are few workers to do the picking. Evangelists, church planters, teachers and youth workers, are just some of the labourers desperately needed. In the developed countries we are spoilt with more than our fair share of Christian labourers. We need to give some away. Eighty per cent of all unreached peoples today, may only meet Jesus Christ through the ministry of cross-cultural missionaries. If the missionaries are not there to work alongside the national churches, thousands may die without having heard about Christ.

Jesus, however, wants to send out workers. Not idlers, sightseers, adventurers or seekers after glory. Labourers get their hands dirty; they do a lot of hard work, and they get the job done. We are not going to become labourers for Jesus overnight. It takes years to develop the character and relationships, and attain the spiritual and academic qualifications that are so vital in Jesus' workforce. Labourers need to be fully prepared and equipped for the job that Jesus has for them.

Your relationship with Jesus

It is important that Jesus is your Lord. Only a person who

has fully surrendered himself to Jesus and is ready to serve him unreservedly will do. You must get to the point where you are willing to obey Christ's commands whether you feel like it or not; whether you agree with them or not. This will hurt at times and will be difficult, but it will pay off when you are facing all sorts of pressures on the front line.

As a cross-cultural missionary you will also need to enjoy fellowship with Jesus and have a deep sensitivity to the leading of the Holy Spirit. Above everything else you must have a desire to see Jesus glorified. Only a person who is willing to lay down his life for the sake of his master will do (1 John 3:16). To help you attain these spiritual qualities consider the following preparations:

1. Become a practician. We are familiar with words like salvation, faith, justification, Holy Spirit. Head knowledge alone will get us no-where in the Lord's service. We have to experience these doctrines; they have to become real to us – now.

2. Become a person of faith. Put yourself in difficult situations where you know you will have to trust the Lord. This way you will gradually learn what it means to live by faith, and you will go out as a person of faith, confident that God will do things. Ask God to show you what difficult situations he wants you to trust him in.

3. Become an intercessor. E.M. Bounds says, 'Prayer is striking the winning blow, service is gathering up the results'. To see results in service, one must first learn how to pray; how to intercede.

4. Become a bookworm. I try and read the New Testament once a month, as well as a section of the Old Testament each day. That usually means about an hour of Bible reading a day. I also try and read a devotional book every week. Remember though, the reading of the Bible should come before all other reading.

5. Become a soldier. We need to know what it means to fight in a spiritual war. We need to know our spiritual weapons. Many missionaries return from the field after

their first term, not wanting to return because they didn't go out prepared to fight.

6. Become a practising heir with Christ. Ask the Lord to reveal to you what it means to be seated with Christ in the heavenly places (Eph. 2:6); what it means to abide in Christ (John 15); and what it means to share in his resurrection life (Rom. 6).

7. Become a lover of Jesus. If you draw near to him, he will draw near to you (James 4:8; 2 Chronicles 4:2). Spending time with Jesus is never wasted time. Everything flows out of our relationship with Jesus. To fall in love with him and to know him intimately is at the heart of this relationship.

Your character

David used a small stone to kill Goliath. The stone was picked out of a brook. While it was in the brook it was forced to rub against other stones in the flowing water. As a result the edges were slowly eroded and it became smooth. It was this smooth stone that helped defeat one of God's enemies.

You need to become like the stone in the brook. As you rub shoulders with other people, your rough edges will be knocked off. As a result the fruit of the Spirit (the smoothness) will be more evident in your life, and you will become the kind of person that God can use to defeat his enemies. Being humble, conscientious, patient, flexible, unselfish and having the ability to work with others as well as having a sense of humour, will gradually characterise your life.

It is for this reason that fellowship with other believers is so important. I am not talking about social gatherings or superficial relationships. If we want to grow and become mature people, we need to learn how to be open, honest and vulnerable with one another. There is no other way. It will hurt, and you will at times be misunderstood, but through it all you will become the kind of person God can use. The small group setting is the ideal 'brook' to develop these types of relationships.

Colin Harrington, a friend of mine who was used by God in Indonesia for twenty years, once told me that the best people to spend time with are the most difficult. You can't help but mature in such company.

Your mind and time

Any one of these would be useful in your academic and practical preparation:

1. Get to know your Bible well. Understand the major doctrines. Read up on church history, systematic theology and apologetics.

2. Obtain a qualification for a useful occupation such as a teacher, nurse, builder, engineer, artist, journalist, secretary.

3. If you can, take a university course in linguistics, anthropology or sociology.

4. If you are working with a business firm, take part-time courses in administration and management.

5. Do a Bible correspondence course. Read books on missions.

6. If you are in the middle of a training course then finish it.

7. Touch up on your English grammar. Attempt to learn a foreign language.

8. Develop the art of writing, photography, typing, speech, book-keeping.

9. Institute a savings plan. Begin to put aside money for training or travelling.[1]

10. Use your holidays to join a short term evangelistic or training programme like YWAM, OM, etc.

Your ministry

In the Early Church it was the experienced minsters who

were sent out as missionaries. Paul, Barnabas, Silas and Timothy had all gained experience in their own churches before being sent out. Any of the following suggestions would help you to be effective in any ministry the Lord may lead you into:

1. Make yourself available for ministry in your own church. Don't go for the big 'up-front' ministry positions initially, but start by assisting your Bible class leader, teach in the Sunday school, teach the Bible in schools, give your testimony, pray aloud, or help out with the administration of your church.

2. Try to find an avenue of ministry which will especially involve teaching. In overseas work, whether you are a mechanic or a pastor, you are often called upon to do some form of teaching.

3. Attend training classes. If your pastor is holding classes in Bible basics, witnessing or leadership – then go to them all. Never stop learning from others.

4. In your participation in church activities, look out for the one in which you find the most fulfillment. This could indicate your spiritual gift and so give possible direction regarding future services.

5. If no sphere of ministry opens up in your local church consider becoming involved with an interdenominational group such as: Open Air Campaigners, Navigators, ISCF, or Youth for Christ.[2]

Your waiting time

Michael Griffiths says, 'There is a real danger that those bitten by "a missionary bug" will spend all their time thinking about the future and neglecting the present.'[3]

It's good to have dreams, but just dreaming about dreams will get us no-where. If we want to see our dreams come true, we need to set goals and make plans now. Before William Carey left for India he studied Hebrew, Greek, Latin, French, Dutch and Italian. His main work in

India was translating the New Testament into the languages of the Indian people. His previous training in languages prepared him for his life-work.

Hudson Taylor had a burning desire to see the Chinese come to Christ. To help realise that dream he began to learn medicine, for he knew it would be a useful means of reaching the Chinese. Also, while in England, he deliberately went without money, food, and other resources, just to see his Lord provide. He wanted to go out as a man of faith, not a potential man of faith.

Jim Elliot was killed by the Auca Indians in Ecuador. However, prior to his leaving for Ecuador he settled the question of the Lordship of Christ in his own life. He came to the point where he was prepared to die for his Lord if need be.

These three men made maximum use of their waiting time, so that their ultimate service for the Lord might be more effective. They experienced the following truths expressed by Michael Griffiths in his book *Give Up Your Small Ambitions:*

'The difficult experiences of the present toughen us and prepare us for the harder experiences to come... without today's shaping, tomorrow's serving would not be possible.'

We come down to the fact that the missionary cannot give what he does not have. He cannot effectively teach the truths he has not experienced himself. The instrument of God must be fully prepared. We must seek to be now, what we want to become tomorrow. Waiting time is such important preparation.

18
Why Training?

The question is so often asked, 'If Hudson Taylor and C.T. Studd and others went out without any formal training, why can't I?' It is true that these men went out with a heart that was ready, willing and full of faith, but they and many others in their time also went out well educated and prepared.

The Apostle Paul, one of the greatest missionaries ever, was a well qualified man. At one time he sat at the feet of Gamaliel, the finest theologian in Jerusalem. As a result he had a thorough knowledge of Hebrew, the Old Testament Scriptures and Jewish culture. He was a skilled rabbinical scholar. He also had some knowledge of Greek thought. Not only was he acquainted with Grecian literature, but also the philosophy of the Stoics. He could speak three languages: Hebrew, the Aramaic vernacular and the colloquial Greek. And we must not forget that he was a trained tent maker. All in all quite a qualified man.[1]

After his conversion he spent about three years in the desert. It was probably during this time that he read and re-read the Scriptures, in light of his conversion to Christ. In a sense, this time was his Bible school. It is not surprising that after this kind of educational background Paul could effectively communicate to the Jews, the Greeks and the Gentiles. He was a man well prepared to speak to his age, he was equipped for the task of being a cross-cultural missionary.

Missions and national churches overseas are not only wanting men and women of faith, but also those who are well equipped, well educated and prepared. Here are the thoughts of two missionary authorities:

Edward Dayton, author and mission professor – 'To go overseas without anthropology, cross-cultural communication training, area studies, missionary life at work – to say nothing of the history of missions and non-Christian religions – is an act of consummate folly. There is probably no profession which requires a higher level of commitment, education and spiritual insight.'[2]

Michael Griffiths, author and world authority on missions – 'It is sometimes overlooked that half the Great Commission is concerned not with making disciples and baptising them, but teaching them everything that Jesus commanded us to. A general knowledge not only of the whole Bible, but also of church history, theology, Christian apologetics, is obviously essential for effective evangelism and teaching, and the best way to get this for most people is to attend a well recommended Bible college or seminary.'[3]

What kind of training?

The Long Corridor
The applicant goes to Bible college for a two year course, with an optional third year. He finds the course valuable and decides to stay on for the third year. He does not waste time, but on completion of his course he applies to the Nameless Missionary Society (NMS) and is accepted for the Candidate's Orientation Programme. He follows this with some Missionary Orientation Courses and the Summer Institute of Linguistics. He spends about a year

with his local church. He is now ready to proceed to the field for a year of language study and orientation. Six years have passed before he settles into a ministry on the field.

The Short Corridor

The applicant enters a crash discipleship course. It lasts six months, during which time he has to rough it, learn to work with others on the course as a team, and receive Bible teaching and missionary orientation. Some mission societies may accept him straight away for cross-cultural ministry. Others may require the applicant to do a further four to twelve months in their Candidate Orientation Course. Either way the applicant reaches the field very quickly.

The Different Corridor

Missionary training can be compared with medical training. In New Zealand, the student must first of all do an intermediate year at a university. After this year, if he has been accepted, he then goes on to medical school for two years. Here both the practical and the theory are combined. From medical school he goes to work in the hospital for another two years. After these two years he becomes a qualified doctor. But some do another two years as a house surgeon before they embark on their chosen field.

Pre-requisites and acceptance qualifications were needed. The theoretical aspects were covered. Practical demonstration was included. Time was given to 'on the job' training. And finally there were the two years of actually doing the job. The 'doctor of souls' requires just as much preparation as the one who cares for the body.

Most of the traditional mission societies require applicants to have done the 'long corridor'. Others, like Youth With A Mission and Operation Mobilisation provide six month discipleship courses and then channel accepted workers into ministry. Some of the old and new mission societies are taking a fresh look at the whole training issue, and as a result, are gradually beginning to implement the 'different corridor'. There is a place for all three 'corridors' and God is definitely blessing them all. Factors that may determine your 'corridor' may include your prospective missionary society, your background, and your personality.

Preparation for Bible college

Here are a few suggestions:
* Build relationships with people.
* Get involved in church activities.
* Read through the whole Bible.
* Aim to lead people to Christ.
* Begin a savings plan to help pay college expenses.
* Keep in touch with training institutions, and find out their entry requirements.

A lot of senior school students, as well as graduating university students, ask, 'Should I work for a year before going to a Bible college, or should I go to college immediately and work my way through?' Both of these options have their advantages and disadvantages. The choice is really determined by the college you want to go to, and the type of person you are.

If you decide to work for a year before going to college, then remember you are in the workforce earning your way, drawing a paycheck, and meeting people of every kind. It is thus a helpful and maturing time. It gives you an opportunity to learn how to look after money and use it wisely. It teaches you how to get along with people. You broaden your view of life in general, as you are exposed to the real needs of ordinary people. If you have really been called by God to go overseas there should be no danger of losing your vision, and in the process you will learn much that will later prove an advantage.

On the other hand, if you decide to go straight to college God may ask you to go with very little money of your own and trust him to provide what you need. Doing this you become an instant student of faith. But it is important that you know God is calling you to do this and that you also have the support of your spiritual elders.

The important thing to remember is that if you are seeking God's will, then however he leads you, it will be good, acceptable and perfect (Romans 12:2).

What type of training is needed?

Our minds are not the only things that need to be trained. In most colleges the majority of the day is spent in lectures, while the evening is taken up with further study. What results is an active mind, and even that is suspect at times, but the person himself can end up dull and boring, with very little spiritual cutting edge. The mind does need to be trained, but so do the spirit, the personality and the body. It is the whole person that ministers, and therefore the whole person needs to receive training. The ideal Bible college should seek to: (a) equip the student; (b) emphasise and give time to the deepening of the student's relationship with God; (c) provide a setting for close personal relationships; and that means, staff with student, and student with student; (d) allow the student to pursue physical and practical interests, like trades and sport.

What I am talking about is lifestyle training. Every single aspect of the student and his lifestyle should be affected by the training. For example, time usage, money, clothes, attitudes, relations to the opposite sex, sleeping habits, reading habits and recreation pursuits. A person can have all the zeal in the world when it comes to serving his Lord, but if he doesn't know how to live a godly life, he will be an ineffective missionary. Godliness is a result of training (1 Tim. 4:7), and, for many, a Bible college provides the setting for such training.

I attended the Worldwide Evangelisation Crusade Missionary Training College in Tasmania, Australia. The course lasted for two years, with an optional third year. The kind of preparation they offered was as follows:

1. Discipleship in a Caring Community
* Fellowship in a family that prays and praises together.
* Exposure to the practical implications of God's word.
* Rubbing shoulders with staff and fellow students.
* Learning a disciplined lifestyle with regard to food, time and relationships.
* Willingness to take correction and guidance towards spiritual maturity.

2. Stretching the Mind.
* Getting to know the Bible by guided personal research.
* Studying: Old Testament, New Testament, Church history, systematic theology, practical theology, missiology, science of religion, biblical ethics, Christian education, and language study.
* Assignments, lectures, films, discussions, plays, group activities are all used.

3. Practical Experience in Service to Non-Christians, Churches, Fellow-Workers.
* All students teach Religious Education classes.
* Three-week missions in the third term.
* Youth groups, Sunday school classes, church services.
* Visitation evangelism.
* Four half-hours per week in building, trades, maintenance, cleaning or gardening – Christian servanthood.
* Opportunities for holiday outreaches.
* Regular prayer for cross-cultural evangelism.
* Daily duties.
* Exercise and sporting activities.

Choosing the place of training

1. Get the details of several colleges and ask God to guide you to the right one. Make this a matter of daily prayer.
2. Get the advice of mature men and women.
3. Get the advice of contemporaries who have studied at

some of the places under review.

4. Take the time to discover the emphases and the doctrinal position of the colleges. (I once knew a couple who went to a college overseas and had to return a few months later, as the emphases of the college were essentially opposed to their own!)

5. Take into account your own background and abilities. This will avoid wasting time studying at a college with a syllabus that is too basic.

6. Don't let negative rumours influence your decision. It is very difficult to get a realistic appraisal of a place from one person who has a few gripes to make about the place. If I had listened to all the negative rumours about the college I finally chose, I would never have gone.

7. Remember you will never find the perfect college. If you think you have, the moment you join it, it will become imperfect! What you consider the weaknesses of the college may provide an ideal opportunity for you to learn to live with a system that you might not fully agree with. You can rest assured that while overseas, you will have to live with many things that you cannot agree with.

8. Don't let the discipline of a Bible college put you off. When a recruit joins the army he has to submit to a whole lot of rules and regulations, and it's all for a purpose. The discipline may be irksome but it is not bad. We need to see beyond the rules, to try and discover why they are there. Overseas you will not be able to do just as you like. You will have to submit to customs and conventions of a different culture. If you are not willing to do those things you don't feel like doing at Bible college, then it is likely you will find it very difficult to adapt to a cross-cultural setting.

What to do after training

Again this is a matter for the Lord's guidance. He is a God of variety and therefore what he might direct you to do may be completely different from what he would ask another to do.

For some of you the right step after training is to go back to your church and put into practice what you have learned. This can be an ideal time to experience all types of ministry. Tom and Chris, whom I have already mentioned, have finished their training. They are now working in a pioneer-type situation trying to plant a church. They hope to gain a lot of experience in this before they go to Muslims in the Middle East. Going back to your church also enables you to build strong relationships again with the church folk before it's time to leave again.

Or, God may ask you to return to your previous occupation after graduating. You can still get involved in your local church, practice what you have learnt, be with non-Christians again, and save some money in anticipation of future moves.

Another option is to take a 'candidates course'. This would mean spending time at your prospective mission's headquarters (not all missions insist on this). The course may be about four months long, or possibly longer, and gives the mission leaders an opportunity to assess you.

Or it may be that God will ask you to go on to further training after graduating – perhaps language study; perhaps a higher degree at a graduate school, or some other form of specialised study at a college or university.

19
Mission Societies

Thank God for mission societies. It was they who did most of the cross-cultural evangelism from the time of Constantine right up to the Reformation. Since 1750 it has been the mission societies, pioneered by such men as William Carey, Hudson Taylor and C.T. Studd, who have penetrated cultural boundaries with the gospel. In recent times such movements as Youth With A Mission and Operation Mobilisation, have done much to send thousands of young Christians into the front lines of missionary work.

Today there are evangelistic and church planting missions. Service agencies such as Gospel Recordings, the Bible Society and the Leprosy Mission are providing valuable help to millions. There are specialist ministries such as aviation, literature, radio, youth and children's work as well as relief agencies like World Vision, Tear Fund and Heed. However, because there are many different kinds of mission society today, it can be a difficult job to decide which one is for you. When making this important decision you should take into account the following factors: the leading of the Lord; the advice of your pastor and elders; the doctrinal position of the mission; does the mission need your particular gifts or ministry? (it is no use joining a medical mission if you have a burden to lecture in a college overseas); do you satisfy the acceptance prerequisites of the mission? Has the mission got a good and godly reputation in all areas? And is the authority structure of the mission one that I feel comfortable in?

Local churches

Thank God for local churches. It was they who made massive inroads into the Jewish and Gentile world during the Apostolic period. Throughout the centuries the churches have provided personal, financial and prayer support to missions.

I particularly want to draw attention to the worldwide church growth movement. Local churches are reaching the lost around them while implementing very successful church growth strategies. As a result churches of 500, 1000, and even 10,000 or more members, have come into being. These churches have the financial base and other resources to launch their own missionary programme in other countries.

Members of these churches have to decide whether to go out with their church or with one of the mission societies. I often hear members of big churches question the scriptural validity of mission societies. Many believe they only came into being because the church wasn't doing its job. Now they ask, 'Since the church has begun to do its job, is there any more need for mission societies?'.

Are mission societies biblical?

Ralph D. Winter, of the U.S. Centre of World Missions, states that there are two types of structures for God's redemptive mission.[1] The first are congregational structures, which he calls modalities, and the second are missionary structures, called sodalities. I agree with him that both are a part of God's Church. It is for this reason that I have chosen not to use the term parachurch to describe mission societies. The word parachurch means 'alongside of the church' and implies that it is not the church itself.

A congregation is a people-orientated structure. A local church should be concerned with equipping the saints for the work of service, and with caring for one another. The local church is essentially a place of healing and growth. The mission structure, however, is a task-orientated structure. By definition, a mission society must select Christians from local churches who are specifically gifted for its task. No-one is born into it. All members have to apply to be accepted. It has a unique and distinct function that all its members serve. (2)

We find examples of task-orientated structures in 1 Samuel 10:10 (a 'band of prophets') and in 19:20 ('the company of the prophets').(3) A similar group is mentioned in connection with Elisha in 2 Kings 2:3 - 4:44. Elisha on the death of Elijah was to be the leader of the 'sons of the prophets.' On one occasion 100 of them met at Gilgal. In the New Testament the formation of a missionary band is mentioned in Acts 13, where Barnabas, Paul, John (Mark) and friends (v. 13) are all included. Charles Mellis, in his book *Committed Communities* writes 'these bands weren't static or inflexible; team composition was in flux. Luke was in-and-out of Paul's team. So, apparently were Timothy, Titus and John Mark. There apparently was communication and fellowship between teams even when they were going separate ways.'(4)

The temple co-existed with the 'band of prophets'. The early house churches co-existed with the missionary bands, and so it is today. The churches co-exist with the mission societies. Both have been and still are a part of the Church. Both have an essential role in God's redemptive plan.

Unfortunately, the relationship between churches and

the mission societies has not always been healthy. Both have tended to go their separate ways. As a result, we have autonomous, missionless churches on one hand, and on the other autonomous churchless missionary societies. Peter Wagner writes, 'that in order to accomplish the mission of the Church, sodalities and modalities need each other in a symbiotic relationship. The symbiotic relationship means that each one contributes to the well-being of the other'.[5] Churches can provide mission societies with leadership, vision and guidance, be used as a means of renewal, and of course provide personal, financial and prayer support. Mission societies can in turn help to renew the churches, educate and challenge them to the plight of the lost and needy, and put to work the trained and equipped church member.

Are mission societies essential ?

Church history reveals that even when churches have been doing their job, there has still been a need for task-oriented mission societies. One of the main reasons is that they have the history and experience in cross-cultural ministry, but local churches do not. It is too simplistic to think that it's just a matter of sending a person or a team of workers over to another country on board a plane. Many other issues are involved. For example, many countries are looking for credibility before they allow a person(s) to enter their country. One person from a local church in a distant country does not have this!

Further, sending over a person or a team and expecting them to start from scratch is in most cases absurd, irresponsible and unrealistic. Why not feed them into a mission society that is already working in the same place, and which has built up resources and openings?

If you are a member of a church that has its own missionary programme in other countries and God is directing you to be involved in this, then that is God's best for you. However if God is asking you to go with another mission society, do not be afraid to discuss this fully with your pastor. If you have not yet decided which, the organisations listed on page 170 will give some guidelines.

Moving out

As soon as someone mentions overseas work, most of us automatically think of missionary work, but thankfully God isn't limited like that. God is a God of variety, as well as of surprises. He sends people out to do many different things, and as times change he also creates new jobs so the task of world outreach is done.

Is everyone a missionary?

In these days of generalisations, some Christians glibly state that they are 'missionaries' because they are involved in some kind of evangelistic work. We have failed to see the distinction between being a missionary and a witness. The Bible, for example, makes it quite clear that we should all teach the truth in love, but that doesn't mean we are all teachers. Likewise, we all have an obligation to witness, but that doesn't automatically mean we are missionaries.

Peter Wagner makes the point that most Christians are monocultural. They are born, get married and eventually die among only one kind of people. The missionary, however, is the person who has the special ability, given by God, to minister in a second culture. Missionaries don't just go overseas, they are sent over there by the Lord and their local church. They cross cultural barriers and religious lines, in order to occupy new frontiers for Christ. Donald McGavran states that the essential work of the missionary is the 'saving of souls, the baptism of bodies, and the multiplying of churches'.[6]

However, God has provided a variety of gifts and a variety of ministries (1 Cor. 12:4,5) to ensure that the missionary work is done. The key missionary ministries are:

(1) *The Evangelist.* This is the person who travels from place to place, telling non-believers about the good news. He has a special ability from God to do this, so that men and women become Jesus' disciples and responsible members of his Body. Churches are founded by the evangelist.

(2) *The Preacher.* He is a forth-teller, who speaks for God, bringing the truth God has revealed to him. He preaches the word of God in the wisdom and power of the Holy Spirit. He speaks to men so as to edify, exhort, encourage and comfort them (1 Cor. 14:3; Eph. 6:19).

(3) *The Pastor/Teacher.* The pastor is the person who can assume a long-term personal responsibility for the spiritual welfare of a group of believers. A number of pastors have the gift of teaching. As a teacher he can communicate information relevant to the health and ministry of the Church in such a way that others will learn.

A service missionary

When an army goes out to war, many people are needed to support that army as it fights. Supplies have to be packaged and organised, radio links set up and maintained, vehicles repaired, sick men cared for and so on. In similar fashion a variety of people are needed to keep the body of missionaries on the field in a state of fighting fitness and preparedness. For example, on the field a missionary group usually require an accountant, a typist, primary and secondary school teachers if children are involved, a doctor, nurse or chemist. If the missionary enterprise has a literature and printing ministry, then writers, printers, machinists, artists, administrators and salesmen are needed. Engineers, builders and pilots are just a few of the many other types of service missionaries.

It must be stated that this type of missionary service is in no way inferior to the career missionary's work. These workers enable the career missionaries to get on with their job. They are a part of the same body in action.

What is a tentmaker?[7]

Every Christian is called to be a witness. No matter where he works or what job he does. Doctors, labourers, carpenters, lecturers, mechanics, etc. – all must be a witness to the people they work with in their God-given calling. The early church multiplied quickly because ordinary folk – in 'nine-to-five' jobs – saw this as their responsibility.

A tentmaker is simply a Christian who does his job overseas – usually a qualified tradesman or specialist – in order to be a witness in another culture. Some Middle East countries prohibit missionaries crossing their borders, but these same countries are wanting to employ qualified personnel from more developed countries to help them advance. Foreign business concerns are thus gaining entry into these countries. Some Christians are taking advantage of this and using it as a means of gaining entry into the country as 'unofficial missionaries'. They go in to do a job and pass on their expertise, but they also look for any opportunity to witness to their faith. It is these Christians who are called tentmakers, after the example of the Apostle Paul in Corinth (Acts 18:3).

Advantages to tentmaking

1. Such persons are not identified as clergymen, or as paid propagandists of religion.
2. In the course of their work they often meet people who are inaccessible to missionaries.
3. They often have more money than regular missionaries.
4. They go at little or no cost to the church, either at home or overseas.
5. They are free to respond to needs which may not be in the programme of the mission.
6. Tentmakers have access to countries which are closed to regular missionaries.

Disadvantages to tentmaking

1. The agency with which he is working may seek to curtail his testimony and limit religious freedom.
2. Tentmaking usually requires a full-time job and can leave insufficient time to develop relationships, learn the local language, etc.
3. The term of service for a tentmaker is usually limited to one or two years.
4. Some self-supporting witnesses have been accused of being deceptive because they are 'missionaries in disguise'. Some also accuse the tentmaker of having double motives, that of being loyal to their employer but also to their faith.
5. Often tentmakers do not have the support of their churches back home.
6. Many companies segregate their workers into special compounds.
7. Many tentmakers do not go out properly trained to witness in another culture, as does a missionary.

Andrew Dymond, a field partner with the Bible and Medical Missionary Fellowship writes, 'Unless a Christian has some orientation to adaptation and outreach for Christ across cultural barriers, he will usually gravitate to those of his own background in the Western community where English is spoken. The majority of tentmakers thus find it difficult to fulfill their desire for an effective cross-cultural ministry.'

Because of this, the tentmaker also needs to undergo some form of preparation.

Spiritual preparation. One or two years in a Bible college will prove most profitable. He needs to know how to study the Scriptures, how to live by faith and walk in the Spirit. A tentmaker may be self-supporting financially but he cannot be self-supporting spiritually. He needs the prayer support of those back home in his church.

Educational preparation. Before going to the assigned country, read as much as possible about the country, its history, geography, politics and economics. A short course in linguistics may also prove helpful.

Cultural preparation. Culture shock is real. An inability to adapt to the new culture and society has caused many to come home. He needs to go with an attitude of empathy and humility, rather than western superiority. It is important to learn about the manners, customs and superstitions of the new country, and to understand why the people have and need them.

Practical preparation. Looking into such things as visas, cost of living, travel facilities and tax regulations before going can save a lot of problems later on.

The short-term worker

This type of service is for those who have a skill, and who want to give a part of their lives to world outreach in a foreign country. Single people, young couples (preferably without children) and older couples can all find opportunities for short-term work.

For example, Les and Jean Walters, both in their seventies, went out to Papua New Guinea to look after a home for missionaries' children. I read an article where a local church has just raised over £3,000 to send five carpenters to another country to help with a building programme.

Youth With A Mission and Operation Mobilisation provide excellent short-term evangelistic training programmes for all ages, but especially for young single people. Hundreds of young people have described these courses as 'life-changing', and many have consequently chosen long-term missionary work.

20
What Next?

Human beings are rut builders. Once they get into something they like to stay there. There are many diehards and traditionalists in our churches. People don't start with the aim of getting themselves into a rut. They often set out with a vision for something new, or a sense or curiosity, but success in achieving a goal breeds satisfaction and comfort. And with it a new status quo. 'Why change something that is successful?' Before they know it, they are in a rut, and the effort to break free is too great, or too controversial.

God is not a God of ruts. In the Old Testament we are told that when the pillar of cloud or fire moved, the Israelites had to pack up and follow (Exodus 13:21). God is a God on the move. In the New Testament God had to allow a dose of persecution to get the disciples out of Jerusalem and into the surrounding districts and countries. That meant changing their location, their jobs, leaving things behind and starting out afresh.

In both Old and New Testaments God is revealed as one who wants to do 'a new thing'. And that is part of his will for you. 'Therefore, if anyone is in Christ, he is a new creation; the old has gone, the new has come' (2 Cor. 5:17). This process starts at conversion, but it doesn't stop there. God is repeatedly wanting to separate you from the old and bring you into glorious new things.

Complacency and apathy are forms of death. They kill any new move, any new growth. You may be happy and successful with what you are doing but that does not necessarily mean God wants you to stay doing that. Being happy and successful does not automatically imply that you are in the centre of God's will. It is when you are obedient to God's voice, that you are in the centre of his will.

You may be entering a time when you are finally coping with a certain ministry and beginning to see much fruit. It has taken you a number of years, and many hours of trial and error, to be where you are now. You think you can begin to relax and enjoy your ministry, but perhaps God wants to take you onto something new. Your successful ministry now may be a preparation for something bigger later on. God wants to take you to your limits. He wants you to be doing something that you know you can't handle without him. He wants you always to be a disciple, that is, a learner. The day you stop learning is the day you begin to backslide. In order to continually learn, God will bring new things along your path.

God is a big and an abundant God. His will for you is so much more than what you think it is. So often we can settle for second best. We can become settled and content with what we are doing and miss out on everything else God intends for us. Don't let that happen to you. His plans for you are big. You may think you are too little for the task. You're right, you are. But remember you have a big God to help you fulfill his big plans.

I have already shared our bewilderment when God asked us to leave what seemed like a successful ministry in New Zealand to go overseas. The church I pastored was packed on most Sunday mornings. The evening congregation had increased four times over. The membership had increased by about 26% and we were beginning to see conversions every month. The church had become the fastest growing Baptist church in the district, when people believed that Baptist churches couldn't grow in that part of the country.

So why has God taken us from a thriving work in New Zealand? Surely we could do more to extend his kingdom here than we could by going to a foreign country? Had we discerned God's guidance rightly? These questions have presented themselves many times since we made the decision to go.

Going overseas as a single man wouldn't be so bad. But the thought of taking my wife and our two-year-old daughter overseas frightens me. To make things worse Robyn is expecting our second child in another few months. We will be subjecting a little baby to the noise, heat and sickness of an Asian city. For the sake of our children and our own comfort we would rather stay in New Zealand.

But God's guidance has been quite clear and specific. When Robyn and I became Christians we made him our Lord. Jesus Christ was to be in charge, what he said we would follow. The cost in going overseas, especially to an Asian city, is very real. But we faced the cost of discipleship at conversion, so now it is not such a big issue. We can look at the environmental and material hardships and know that in some ways it will be hard, and it is tempting to get miserable at times. But we also know there is more misery in being disobedient to God's good, pleasing and perfect will.

I will hardly be missed in leaving New Zealand. There will be someone to take my place. But in many other countries around this needy world, national leaders are crying out for at least one or two missionaries. People say that the need does not constitute the call. That's partly correct. We need to know whether that need has our name on it. But I agree with Brother Andrew when he states, 'a call is to know about a need. Too many Christians say "I have no call". But I say that you have never heard the call, because God has called you. He has told you to get acquainted with the need in the world'.

Finally, in the West we are so 'work output' orientated. What we do and how much we do is what counts. In our churches we have adopted this spirit of the world and let church growth, evangelism, outreach or whatever you want to call it become too important. We have made Christian work one of the prime reasons we are in existence. That is not biblical.

'In him we were also chosen, having been predestined according to the plan of him who works out everything in conformity with the purpose of his will, in order that we, who were the first to hope in Christ, might be for the praise of his glory' (Eph. 1: 11,12).

Primarily, what counts to God is not whether we are working hard for him and extending his kingdom, but whether we are bringing glory to him. One of my biggest doubts about going overseas was that surely I could extend his kingdom more here in New Zealand by helping this Baptist church to grow. I began to see, however, that God doesn't place us here or there just to extend his kingdom. He takes us to places so that in our going and being there we can glorify him. I don't know how we can glorify God in a foreign city, but God does.

I have now been a Christian for eight years. In that time I have worked in a paper bag factory, been a part-time church worker, a full-time youth worker, spent two years at a Bible college, and three years in full-time pastoral work. And now I am off abroad to do missionary work. After that, only God knows. There is nothing impressive about my past eight years; I have only done what I believed God was calling me to do. But looking at my brief Christian history I can see that God never allowed me to get into a nice, comfortable, successful rut. There was always something more; there was always a new road with God.

I believe that's the way it is meant to be. I am not suggesting that you give up your job and do what I have done. I am talking about a principle and God will work out that principle in your life that will be different from mine. God may call you to stay in your job until you retire, but you can do that without finding yourself in a rut. God wants to reveal new aspects of his character to you. He wants to change you. He wants you to pray, study the Bible and worship in new ways. He wants to bring across your path new friends and new challenges. He wants to change your ministry so you are continually learning new ways of serving and helping people. He wants you to see the world in a new way and perhaps have a new ministry in world evangelism. There is so much more he wants to do in and through your life

'Now to him who is able to do immeasurably more than all we ask or imagine, according to his power that is at work within us, to him be glory in the church and in Christ Jesus throughout all generations, for ever and ever! Amen.' (Eph. 3: 20,21).

Notes

Chapter One
1. David B. Barrett, *World Christian Encyclopedia*, Oxford University Press, 1982.
2. WEC *Worldwide*, Mar/Apr. 1983 issue, WEC Press.
3. Pico Iyer, *Time*, July 11 1983 issue.
4. Michael Griffiths, *World Mission in the Eighties*, STL, 1980.
5. *Time*, 'A Cry for Leadership', Aug. 6 1979 issue.

Chapter Two
1. Michael Green, *You Must Be Joking*, Hodder & Stoughton, 1976.
2. Edward Dayton & David Fraser, *Planning Strategies for World Evangelisation*, Eerdmans, 1980.
3. Ibid.
4. Ibid.
5. Ibid.

Chapter Five
1. Jamie Buckingham, *The Last Word*, Logos, 1978.
2. Taken from David Watson's foreword to Ron Sider's, *Rich Christians in an Age of Hunger*, Hodder & Stoughton, 1977.

Chapter Six
1. Juan Carlos Ortiz, *Disciple*, Creation House, 1975.
2. Ron Sider, *Rich Christians in an Age of Hunger*, Hodder & Stoughton, 1977.

Chapter Seven
1. Lloyd Cory, *Quote Unquote*, Victor Books, 1977.
2. David Watson, *I Believe in the Church*, Hodder & Stoughton, 1978.

3. Michael Green, *I Believe in the Holy Spirit*, Hodder &
    Stoughton, 1975.
4. Andrew Murray, *Key to the Missionary Problem*, CLC,
    1979.

Chapter Nine
1. Brother Andrew, *Building in a Broken World*,
    Tyndale, 1981.
2. Michael Griffiths, *Don't Soft Peddle God's Call*, OMF,
    1975.
3. George Peters, *A Biblical Theology of Missions*,
    Moody Press, 1972.
4. Brother Andrew, *Building in a Broken World*,
    Tyndale, 1981.

Chapter Ten
1. Peter Wagner, *Your Spiritual Gifts*, Regal, 1979.
2. Ibid.
3. Ibid.

Chapter Eleven
Time, May 31, 1982; Vol. 119, No.22.

Chapter Twelve
1. Marjorie Collins, *Who Cares about the Missionary*,
    Moody Press, 1974.
2. Paul Billheimer, *Destined for the Throne*, CLC
3. Stewart Dinnen, *20 Points on Praying for
    Missionaries*, WEC Press.
4. C.H. Spurgeon, *Barbed Arrows*, Baker Book House,
    1980.

Chapter Thirteen
1. *Leadership Magazine*, Article by Terry Muck, Winter
    1982, Vol. 111, No.1, Christianity Today.
2. Richard Foster, *Celebration of Discipline*, Hodder &
    Stoughton, 1978.
3. David Bryant, *In The Gap*, IVM, 1979.
4. Andrew Murray, *Key to The Missionary Problem*, CLC
    1975.

Chapter Fourteen

1. Lloyd Cory, *Quote Unquote*, Victor Books,1977.
2. Billy Graham, *The Quotable Billy Graham*, Murray, 1967.
3. David Pawson, *Tapes on Giving*, Inspirational Tapes.
4. Ron Sider, *Rich Christians in an Age of Hunger*, Hodder & Stoughton, 1977.
5. Marjorie Collins, *Who Cares About the Missionary?*, Moody Press, 1974.

Chapter Fifteen

1. Lloyd Cory, *Quote Unquote*, Victor Books, 1977.
2. Floyd McLung, *Friendship Evangelism*, YWAM.

Chapter Sixteen

1. R.E. Reeves, *Where Will Mission Minded Pastors Come From?*, Global Church Growth Bulletin, V.XVII, No.4.
2. Michael Griffiths, *Get Your Church Involved In Missions*, OMF Books.

Chapter Seventeen

1. Stewart Dinnen, *After Committment What?*, WEC.
2. Ibid.
3. Michael Griffiths, *Give Up Your Small Ambitions*, IVP.

Chapter Eighteen

1. Edward R. Dayton, David A. Fraser, *Planning Strategies for World Evangelisation*, Eerdmans, 1980.
2. Ibid.
3. Ibid.

Chapter Nineteen

1. Ralph D. Winter, *Perspectives on the World Christian Movement*, William Carey Library, 1983.
2. C.P. Wagner, *Leading Your Church to Growth*, Regal, 1984.

3. Charles Mellis, *Committed Communities*, William Carey Library, 1976.
4. Ibid.
5. C.P. Wagner, *Leading Your Church to Growth*, Regal, 1984.
6. George Peter, *A Biblical Theology of Missions*, Moody Press, 1972.
7. J. Christy Wilson, *Today's Tentmakers*.

Further Information

Recommended reading

The Challenge of Missions, Oswald J. Smith, STL Books, 1983.

The Christian at Work Overseas, edited by Ian Prior, TEAR Fund, 1976.

Don't Just Stand There, Martin Goldsmith, STL Books, 1976.

Eternity in Their Hearts, Don Richardson, Regal Books, 1981.

How Are You Doing?, Stewart Dinnen, STL Books, 1984.

Key to the Missionary Problem, Andrew Murray, CLC, 1979.

A Lion Handbook of the World's Religions, Lion Publishing, 1982.

Love Your Local Missionary, edited by Martin Goldsmith, STL Books, 1984.

On the Crest of the Wave, C. Peter Wagner, Regal Books, 1983.

Operation World, Patrick Johnstone, STL Books, 1978.

Perspectives on the World Christian Movement, edited by Ralph D. Winter with Steven C. Hawthorne, William Carey Library, 1981.

Ten Sending Churches, edited by Michael Griffiths, STL Books, 1985.

What on Earth Are You Doing?, Michael Griffiths, IVP, 1983.

World Missions – Total War, L. E. Maxwell, Prairie Press, 1977.

Magazines

The following periodicals will also prove to be a valuable source of information and challenge:

Evangelical Missions Quarterly , Box 794, Wheaton, Illinois 60189, USA

FACTS (published 3 times a year), Active Christian Training Service, 119 Marlborough Park South, Belfast, BT9 6HW.

The Wider LOOK (quarterly), 68 Summerleaze Road, Maidenhead, Berkshire, SL6 8EP, UK.

World Christian (quarterly) PO Box 40010, Pasadena, California 91104, USA.

Many missionary societies have their own regular magazines – for addresses see *Operation World* (listed above) or the *UK Christian Handbook* (MARC Europe).

Further enquiries

These organisations will be happy to respond to your queries about missionary opportunities:

In-Service Program, Fuller School of World Mission, 135 N. Oakland Avenue, Pasadena, California 91101, USA.

Intercristo Center for Christian Work Opportunities, Box 33487, Seattle, Washington 98133, USA.

TEMA, Route d'Echallens 34, 1032 Romanel-sur-Lausanne, Switzerland.

Evangelical Missionary Alliance, Whitefield House, 186 Kennington Park Road, London, SE11 4BT, UK.

Going Places

Preparing for Christian service

Elizabeth Goldsmith

It lingers in the back of your mind. The thought that God might one day call you to work for him 'full-time'. At home or abroad, short or long term, in the church or some other kind of Christian work – who knows?

But how will I know if God does call me? What kind of person does he want? And ought I to be doing something about it now?

Elizabeth Goldsmith, for ten years an overseas missionary and now in this country helping train others for Christian service, answers these questions and gives lots of practical advice for those who want to be 'going places' for God.

Published jointly with Inter-Varsity Press

 STL Books

Ten Sending Churches

Ten ministers share how they and their
churches have caught the vision for mission

Edited by Michael Griffiths

Support for mission is part of most churches'
life, but is it really effective? Here are ten
churches, from different areas and traditions,
which are taking mission to their hearts.

Ideas for raising interest, examples of
thoughtful enterprise, imaginative backing for
individuals – all are shared, with a wealth of
other suggestions. The ministers write with
refreshing honesty, offering new insights and
innovations, and helping to answer the
question which **Jim Graham** of Gold Hill
Baptist raises: 'How can we, as a church,
release more and more resources into the
harvest fields of the world?'

Published jointly with MARC Europe and EMA

 STL Books

Love Your Local Missionary

Edited by Martin Goldsmith

Christians pay lip service to the goal of mission, but commit little money or time. Yet many are called to the mission field: over 5,500 from Britain alone are serving with different societies. How can the churches help?

Love Your Local Missionary explains how Christians can understand the vital importance of mission and offer friendship, prayer and support where it is most needed.

Martin Goldsmith, lecturer at All Nations Christian College, writes on the biblical basis of mission; the **Rev. Stanley Davies**, General Secretary of the Evangelical Missionary Alliance, surveys missionary outreach today; the **Rev. John Wallis**, Home Director of the Overseas Missionary Fellowship, describes how to back the missionary abroad; and **Dr Anne Townsend**, editor of *Family* magazine, shows how local Christians can offer help where it is needed to the missionary at home.

Published jointly with MARC Europe and EMA

STL Books

A Hitch-hiker's Guide to Mission

Ada Lum

For many years, Ada Lum's job whisked her around Asia with her baby typewriter, her entire home and office in one suitcase. She discovered that mission means both the making of disciples and encounter across cultures.

She had originally expected to go to China. Much to her surprise, Ada Lum ended up on an adventure that would take her from Hawaii to Hong Kong to Pakistan to Brazil to London and back to Hawaii again.

With wit and wisdom, Ada Lum vividly challenges and encourages all who are considering God's call to mission anywhere, whether at home or further afield. The book is as lively as its author.

A Hawaiian Chinese, Ada Lum joined the Internatonal Fellowship of Evangelical Students in Hong Kong in 1962. Her itinerant East Asian ministry lasted from 1968 to 1977, after which she became IFES Bible Study Secretary, a role which took her to all continents, training students and leaders.

Published jointly with Inter-Varsity Press

STL Books

My Big Father

Dr Bruce Farnham

Although from an often persecuted religious minority group, **Kenan Araz** had a fervent desire to share the love of his 'Big Father' with his Muslim neighbours.

When kidney disease threatened him with certain death, his 'Big Father' intervened in a marvellous way. The unusual result – living with three kidneys – provided Kenan with a unique opening for personal witness during the remaining few years of his life.

Yet Kenan's biography is more than just the story of a life laid down. It is also the story of the church in Turkey, that has itself fallen into the ground and died many times during its long and painful history.

STL Books

Mountain Rain

A new biography of James O Fraser

Eileen Crossman

James had a quickened sense that people were praying for him at home. Thousands of miles away, they were directly engaged in the work of God among the Lisu, and concerned too in keeping James himself filled with the Spirit of power. He knew conclusively now that the prayers of God's people had brought the harvest.

James Fraser was only twenty-two when he went to China. At first sight of the Lisu tribespeople of Yunnan province he felt an immediate affection for them, and for the rest of his life he laboured to bring them to Christ and to Christian maturity. His daughter **Eileen Crossman** has brought him to life for today's readers in this superb new biography which reveals the secret of his success.

Published jointly with OMF Books

STL Books